XENOS 1

THE ANCIENT AND THE ELDRITCH

CONTENTS

PRODUCED BY GAMES WORKSHOP IN NOTTINGHAM

With thanks to the Mournival for their additional playtesting services

Games Workshop Ltd, Willow Rd, Lenton, Nottingham, NG7 2WS

games-workshop.com

INTRODUCTION

Welcome to volume one of *Index: Xenos*. This is one of five tomes which together contain updated rules for every unit of miniatures in Warhammer 40,000. If you have an army of Craftworld Eldar, Harlequins, Ynnari, Dark Eldar or Necrons, this volume contains all the information you need to field your models in the new edition of the Warhammer 40,000 game.

Within these pages are detailed rules entries, known as datasheets, for every Citadel Miniature within the Craftworlds, Drukhari, Harlequins, Ynnari and Necron Factions. When taken together with the *Warhammer 40,000* rulebook, you will have everything you need to field these deadly xenos on the battlefield. The knowledge contained inside will enable you to fight for the glories of the Craftworlds, serve the Laughing God, wield the power of death, prey on the lesser races of realspace, or ensure your dynasty ascends to rule the stars once more.

Though the upstart Imperium lays claim to the stars, there exist alien races who ruled the galaxy when Man was still crawling from his caves. Though they have lingered long in the twilight, these races are rising up once more to take what is theirs and re-establish the grandest of empires.

The Aeldari of the Craftworlds seek to master fate itself, twisting the fabric of the future with every act of war until the tapestry of destiny runs in their favour. The warrior dancers of the Harlequins pursue their own mysterious agenda, bringing every power they can to bear against the scourge of Chaos. The Ynnari, called the Reborn for their ability to cheat death, also seek to unite the Eldar race – they use the power of the spirit god Ynnead to stay beyond the clutches of the Aeldari nemesis, Slaanesh. The Drukhari force others to suffer in their stead, raiding the worlds of realspace from their nightmare cities in the webway. All these facets of the Aeldari seek to thrive at Humanity's expense, yet there remains a force darker still. The Necrons are rising from stasis crypts and tomb worlds, an undying menace that will stop at nothing until all other races are enslaved to their will in the name of sterile order.

INSIDE YOU WILL FIND:

- **Army Lists:** The first five sections of this book present all of the datasheets that you will need in order to use your Aeldari or Necron miniatures in games of Warhammer 40,000, along with the additional rules and psychic disciplines that make each of these factions unique.

- **Battle-forged Armies:** This presents a guide on how to organise your miniatures into an army for matched play games, including photocopiable Army Roster sheets.

- **Appendix:** This section contains all of the profiles and rules for the weapons and wargear carried by the units covered in this book, as well as all of the points values you will need to use your army in matched play games.

DATASHEETS

1. Battlefield Role

This is typically used when making a Battle-forged army.

2. Power Rating

The higher this is, the more powerful the unit! You can determine the Power Level of your entire army by adding up the Power Ratings of all the units in your army.

3. Unit Name

Models move and fight in units, which can have one or more models. Here you'll find the name of the unit.

4. Profiles

These contain the following characteristics that tell you how mighty the models in the unit are:

Move (M): This is the speed at which a model moves across the battlefield.

Weapon Skill (WS): This tells you a model's skill at hand-to-hand fighting. If a model has a Weapon Skill of '-' it is unable to fight in melee and cannot make close combat attacks at all.

Ballistic Skill (BS): This shows how accurate a model is when shooting with ranged weapons. If a model has a Ballistic Skill of '-' it has no proficiency with ranged weapons and cannot make shooting attacks at all.

Strength (S): This indicates how strong a model is and how likely it is to inflict damage in hand-to-hand combat.

Toughness (T): This reflects the model's resilience against physical harm.

Wounds (W): Wounds show how much damage a model can sustain before it succumbs to its injuries.

Attacks (A): This tells you how many times a model can strike blows in hand-to-hand combat.

Leadership (Ld): This reveals how courageous, determined or self-controlled a model is.

Save (Sv): This indicates the protection a model's armour gives.

FIRE DRAGONS

NAME	M	WS	BS	S	T	W	A	Ld	Sv
Fire Dragon	7"	3+	3+	3	3	1	1	8	3+
Fire Dragon Exarch	7"	3+	3+	3	3	2	2	8	3+

This unit contains 5 Fire Dragons. It can include up to 5 additional Fire Dragons (Power Rating +6). A Fire Dragon Exarch can take the place of a Fire Dragon. Each model is armed with a fusion gun and melta bombs.

WEAPON	RANGE	TYPE	S	AP	D	ABILITIES
Dragon's breath flamer	8"	Assault D6	5	-1	1	This weapon automatically hits its target.
Firepike	18"	Assault 1	8	-4	D6	If the target is within half range of this weapon, roll two dice when inflicting damage with it and discard the lowest result.
Fusion gun	12"	Assault 1	8	-4	D6	If the target is within half range of this weapon, roll two dice when inflicting damage with it and discard the lowest result.
Melta bomb	6"	Grenade 1	8	-4	D6	You can re-roll failed wound rolls for this weapon when targeting a VEHICLE.

WARGEAR OPTIONS	The Fire Dragon Exarch may replace their fusion gun with a dragon's breath flamer or a firepike.

ABILITIES	**Ancient Doom, Battle Focus** (pg 10)	**Assured Destruction:** You can re-roll wound rolls of 1 in the Shooting phase for attacks this unit make that target MONSTERS or VEHICLES.
	Crack Shot: You can re-roll hit rolls of 1 for a Fire Dragon Exarch's ranged weapons.	

FACTION KEYWORDS	AELDARI, ASURYANI, ASPECT WARRIOR, <CRAFTWORLD>
KEYWORDS	INFANTRY, FIRE DRAGONS

5. Unit Composition & Wargear

This tells you what models are in the unit and covers the basic weapons and equipment the models are armed with.

6. Weapons

The weapons that a unit comes equipped with are described using a set of characteristics as follows:

Range: How far the weapon can shoot. Weapons with a range of 'Melee' can only be used in hand-to-hand combat. All other weapons are referred to as ranged weapons.

Type: These are all explained under the Shooting and Fight phases of the core rules.

Strength (S): How likely the weapon is to inflict damage. If a weapon's Strength lists 'User', it is equal to the wielder's current Strength. If a weapon lists a modifier such as '+1' or 'x2', you should modify the user's current Strength characteristic as shown to determine the weapon's Strength. For example, if a weapon's Strength was 'x2', and the user had a Strength characteristic of 6, that weapon has Strength 12.

Armour Penetration (AP): How good it is at getting through armour.

Damage (D): The amount of damage inflicted by a successful hit.

7. Wargear Options

Some units have a number of choices as to which gear they take into battle – this section describes these options. Weapons which a unit may take as an optional choice are typically described in the appendix.

8. Abilities

Many units have exciting special abilities that are not covered by the core rules; these will be described here.

9. Keywords

All datasheets have a list of keywords, sometimes separated into Faction keywords and other keywords. The former can be used as a guide to help decide which models to include in your army, but otherwise both sets of keywords are functionally the same. Sometimes a rule will say that it applies to models that have a specific keyword. For example, a rule might say that it applies to 'all ORKS models'. This means it would only apply to models that have the Orks keyword on their datasheet.

THE AELDARI

The Aeldari once ruled the stars. Their galactic empire was a utopia of peace and technological wonder, until they were brought low by their own arrogance. Now they are a fragmented race, divided between those who would rage against the dying of the light, and those who embrace the hedonistic cruelty that led to their fall.

Millions of years ago, the Aeldari empire spanned the galaxy, and was filled with wonders beyond count. Entire worlds were created and stars destroyed to satisfy the whims of the Aeldari, and no threat existed that could possibly challenge their dominance. Yet in the end it was not war that spelled their doom, but something far more subtle and insidious. Having outgrown the need for labour and reached the very heights of scientific endeavour, the Aeldari devoted themselves to increasingly obsessive pursuits. Over the course of many thousands of years, this long-lived race began to desire new and ever more extreme experiences. Cults sprang up across the empire that embraced and encouraged this hedonism, and countless Aeldari lost themselves in the pursuit of esoteric knowledge and sensual excess. This moral sickness ran rampant through the Aeldari, and over time corruption of their race coalesced into a gestalt consciousness within the warp – a realm of boundless, roiling energy where the emotions and sensations of sentient beings take on a form and consciousness of their own. Slaanesh, the Dark God of excess, was born.

When Slaanesh finally burst into divine consciousness, a psychic implosion tore at the universe. In a heartbeat, the aeons-old Aeldari civilisation was ripped away, leaving in its place the warp rift that men call the Eye of Terror. Countless billions of Aeldari were consumed by this cataclysm, their souls torn from their bodies and devoured greedily by the newborn god. Only a fraction of this once mighty people escaped. Many Aeldari had already fled the apocalypse they had long suspected was imminent, settling new planets far from the heart of the old empire – these Aeldari called themselves the Exodites, and remained uncorrupted by Chaos. Those that would become the cruel-hearted, sadistic Drukhari were already hidden deep within the labyrinthine tunnels of the webway, while a very few far-sighted Aeldari abandoned the dying empire upon great vessels known as craftworlds, scattering across the vast expanse of space. All were marked by ever-hungry Slaanesh. Should any Aeldari fall from this moment on, their souls were hers to claim.

It is a mark of the willpower of this proud race that in the millennia since the fall, they have not meekly accepted their fate. Though faced on all sides by hostile aliens determined to claim their place as true masters of the galaxy, the Aeldari race fought on. The Asuryani – those Aeldari who remained on craftworlds – and the Exodites embraced the asceticism and spiritual purity that had once defined their race, and fought to preserve the remnants of their lost culture. By utilising the precious crystals known as spirit stones, the Craftworld Aeldari realised they could capture one's spirit essence upon death, preserving the soul in a state of limbo where it could be kept safe from the hunger of Slaanesh. By contrast the Drukhari sank deeper into malicious cruelty. Lurking deep in the webway in the nightmarish city of Commorragh, a sprawling transdimensional metropolis, these sadistic reavers discovered that they could cheat Slaanesh of her due by feeding upon the pain and anguish of others, thus renewing their external youth and beauty even as their hearts became ever more hollow and corrupted. Their raiding parties sally endlessly forth from the webway in search of fresh slaves to agonise.

So did the scattered scions of the Aeldari exist for many millennia, refusing to allow the light of their culture to fade even as the galaxy around them slipped further into madness and ruin. Just when the future of their race seemed at its very darkest, there came an upheaval that shook both the Aeldari of the Craftworlds and the Drukhari to their very core. The nascent deity known as Ynnead, God of the Dead, had been slowly coalescing over thousands of years, growing stronger as the Aeldari suffered through millennia of war and loss. Thanks to the actions of the Ulthwé Farseer Eldrad Ulthran and the prophet Yvraine, the God of the Dead awoke from his slumber far earlier than even the greatest seers had predicted. His awakening spelled momentous change for every Aeldari.

The Ynnari, the worshippers of Ynnead, have learned to act as living infinity circuits, drawing in the souls of the slain which saves the departed from being devoured by Slaanesh, even as it empowers the Ynnari themselves. Indeed, Ynnead's followers believe that his destiny will see the Chaos Gods defeated and their race resurgent once more. Many Aeldari have sworn fealty to the forces of Ynnead's mortal servants. Warriors of the craftworlds and Drukhari reavers alike fight alongside the death god's chosen, their ancient hearts once again afire with rekindled hope. Yet not all share this new-found faith. Factions within the craftworlds see the Ynnari as little more than Chaos-tainted false prophets, and the great lords of Commorragh are loathe to bend the knee before these self-proclaimed saviours. The Ynnari, would-be unifiers of their scattered people, may in fact have splintered the Aeldari more completely than ever.

LABYRINTH OF THE LOST EMPIRE

The webway exists between the material realm and the warp. Created through technologies once taught to the Aeldari by the ancient race known as the Old Ones, its tunnels lead to the craftworlds, to the shadow-shrouded spires of Commorragh, and to untold thousands of other locations. Though the webway still connects many Exodite planets, untouched maiden worlds and craftworlds to one another, the baleful energies of the Fall ruptured many of its hyperspatial pathways. Amongst the webway's shattered and treacherous tendrils there are many dead ends and mazes. Some lead to places long since abandoned, destroyed or infested by the Daemons of the warp. The craftworld seers claim there are many secret paths, though only the elegant Harlequins truly know of their full extent. It is rumoured that a transdimensional map was made thousands of years ago, a priceless artefact now kept in the fabled Black Library, repository of all the Aeldari's eldritch knowledge. Both the warhosts of the Craftworld Aeldari and the reaver-fleets of the Drukhari use the webway to launch rapid assaults against their foes, striking a killing blow before disappearing like vengeful ghosts into the depths of this twisting labyrinth.

CRAFTWORLDS

Vast interstellar arks constructed from living wraithbone, the craftworlds of the Aeldari are marvels of grace and beauty. No less graceful are their occupants, the Asuryani, the noble-hearted Aeldari who foresaw the fall of their empire and escaped its death throes. Even now, they carry the flickering ember of its former glory into an uncertain future.

Swift as rushing water, the Craftworld Aeldari strike. Lithe and impossibly graceful, warriors in wondrous battle-plate leap into the fray, their every motion elegant and utterly deadly. Enemies fall in their droves, cut down by artful strikes and dazzling flourishes. Weaving through the chaos of battle come agile dagger-craft and grav-tanks, circling the crude vehicles of the foe with blinding speed before launching precision volleys of laser fire that detonate enemy armour in blossoming fireballs. The scream of jet engines splits the air as formations of strike craft knife across the sky, shredding enemy fighters into fragments with crackling beams of superheated energy. Outwitted, outmanoeuvred and outfought, the foe is encircled and destroyed with swift and merciless precision. Thus do the Aeldari of the craftworlds make war.

The world-ships which the craftworlders call home were originally created as spacefaring arks by those ancient Aeldari who foresaw the horrifying fate of their empire, and who fled far enough to escape the hunger of She Who Thirsts. Each of the surviving craftworlds represents but a small fragment of that lost civilisation, and within their crystal domes and glittering gardens the Aeldari live their lives as they have done for millennia, following the ascetic Paths that keep them from falling prey to the same decadence as their forebears.

Each craftworld is home to the dead as well as the living. Slaanesh is ever-hungry, and should an Aeldari die their eternal soul falls into her foul embrace. To avoid this awful fate, craftworlders wear objects called waystones upon their person. These psycho-receptive crystals capture the wearer's essence upon death, preventing She Who Thirsts from claiming her due. Should an Aeldari fall, their waystone – known as a spirit stone when it is infused with the spirit essence of its fallen bearer – will be gathered and returned to their craftworld, where the soul within is transferred into the wraithbone infinity circuit of the ancient vessel. In times of great

need the restless dead can be called upon by the living, siphoned from the ship's psychoactive skeleton and interred in a wraithbone war construct. Even in death the Aeldari of the craftworlds fight for the future of their race.

The Craftworld Aeldari are the guardians of their people's culture, history and traditions, forever striving to preserve an echo of its past greatness. The exact number of craftworlds that escaped the Fall is unknown, though there are several that are renowned for their impact upon the wider galaxy. Each pursues its own endeavours and prosecutes war in its own manner, and each still bears its own scars from the Fall so many thousands of years later.

Craftworld Alaitoc wanders the far frontier of the galaxy, on the edge of unexplored space. Far away from the corrupting influence of the Eye of Terror, those of the Alaitoc are driven by a puritanical adherence to the Path. This zealous spirit offers a potent shield against the corrupting touch of Slaanesh, but also causes many of the craftworld's warriors to lose themselves on their chosen Path, becoming the elite warriors known as Exarchs. Many Alaitoc find such ascetic demands overbearing, and embrace the Path of the Outcast. Thus, Alaitoc can call upon a great number of scouts and Rangers when the need arises.

The warriors of the Saim-Hann craftworld are masters of the lightning assault, favouring the rapid deployment of jetbike units and grav-tank formations, falling on their foes with stunning speed and ferocity. Among the first Aeldari to set off aboard their craftworld, the Wild Host are a passionate and hot-tempered force, and many other Aeldari look on them as uncultured and savage. Those of Saim-Hann care not, for they ride together united as blood brothers and sisters, their war-cries echoing above the wail of jetbike engines.

The Aeldari of Craftworld Biel-Tan ever strive to return their race to their former glory, and have pursued many campaigns of xenocide against those races foolish enough to encroach upon the maiden and Exodite worlds that lie beneath their protection. The Biel-Tani are a militant and aggressive people, who place more emphasis upon the Path of the Warrior than any other craftworld – many Aspect Warriors fill the ranks of their armies. When the prophet Yvraine of the Ynnari drew one of the Blades of Power from Biel-Tan's spine, she birthed the mighty Yncarne, but also sundered the world-ship forever. Where once a single, graceful craftworld drifted through the void, now the Biel-Tani dwell upon scattered fleets of spacecraft, fashioned from the shattered remnants of their home. While many of its people saw the Ynnari as their greatest hope of reclaiming their former glory, many others cursed the name of those who had brought such destruction to their home, and refused to fight at their side.

Craftworld Iyanden is a place of death, a grave world where the living walk amidst the tombs of their fallen kindred. Once among the most populous and intrepid of the craftworlds, Iyanden was unfortunate enough to find itself in the path of Hive Fleet Kraken. Countless Aeldari were devoured before the Tyranid menace was finally driven off. Ever since, Iyanden's dead have greatly outnumbered its living. Thus, the craftworld fields a great number of wraithbone constructs, Wraithblades and Wraithguard whose presence ensures that the glory of Iyanden is not forgotten.

The Ulthwé craftworld roams close to the Eye of Terror, and is home to some of the most powerful psykers in the galaxy. The divinations of Ulthwé Farseers have foiled the plots of Chaos and advanced the cause of the Aeldari race on countless occasions, though many other craftworlds still consider the Ulthwé cursed by their proximity to the Eye and call its inhabitants the Damned. Because Ulthwé relies so heavily on its psykers, and because the Path of the Seer is such a time-consuming and dangerous one, the craftworld can spare few of its people to study the Path of the Warrior. Consequently, it counts few Aspect Warriors amongst the ranks of its armies, instead relying upon a standing army of citizen troops known as the Black Guardians, each of whom is a veteran of countless wars against Chaos-warped raiders.

Should the shadow of war fall across a craftworld, its Aspect Warrior shrines, armadas of grav-craft and spirit-driven constructs swiftly make ready for war. Civilians set aside the tools of peace to take up arms as Guardians, the militias which make up the core of the mighty Aeldari warhosts. Though not professional soldiers, each long-lived Guardian is nonetheless the equal of a warrior of another race who has spent their entire life mastering the art of combat. Led by the strategically brilliant Autarchs – Aeldari who have fully embraced the Path of Command – the warhosts of the Craftworld Aeldari strike without warning across the galaxy, piercing the heart of the foe before they are even aware of their peril. Mounted astern of every craftworld is a shimmering webway gate. Linked to an impossibly vast network of tunnels through time and space, this portal allows the Craftworld Aeldari to send their armies and warriors immeasurable distances across the stars. Thus, the location of a craftworld is little hindrance to its armies, as it remains forever connected to the galaxy even when hidden deep within the void.

THE PATH

Aeldari are creatures of soaring passion and heightened sensitivity – both traits which contributed to the downfall of their empire and the birth of their nemesis, Slaanesh. To control and focus these attributes, the Aeldari of the craftworlds turn to a practice steeped in mystical tradition known as the Path, which helps temper the fickle and obsessive nature of their race. Each Aeldari will make a choice from many thousands of Paths, which they follow to the exclusion of all else until it is mastered. They will then move on to another, and another, rarely sticking to a single Path too long lest it eclipse their sense of self. There are many varied Paths – the ways of the Artisan, Voidfarer and Healer are all vital roles within a craftworld, for instance – and for much of their life an Aeldari might pursue perfection in relative peace. However, as the long night draws in and enemies gather in the darkness, more and more Aeldari turn to the Path of the Warrior, their souls tempered in the flames of battle and quenched in blood.

CRAFTWORLDS ARMY LIST

This section contains all of the datasheets that you will need in order to fight battles with your Craftworlds miniatures. Each datasheet includes the characteristics profiles of the unit it describes, as well as any wargear and abilities it may have. Some rules are common to several Craftworlds units – these are described below and referenced on the datasheets.

KEYWORDS

Throughout this section you will come across a keyword that is within angular brackets, specifically <CRAFTWORLD>. This is shorthand for a keyword of your own choosing, as described below.

<CRAFTWORLD>

The Craftworld Aeldari all belong to a craftworld. When you include a craftworld unit in your army, you must nominate which craftworld that unit is from. There are many different craftworlds to choose from; you can use any of the craftworlds described in our books, or make up your own craftworld if you prefer. You then simply replace the <CRAFTWORLD> keyword in every instance on that unit's datasheet with the name of your chosen craftworld.

For example, if you were to include an Autarch in your army, and you decided they were from Craftworld Biel-Tan, then their <CRAFTWORLD> keyword is changed to BIEL-TAN, and their 'The Path of Command' ability would say 'You can re-roll hit rolls of 1 for friendly BIEL-TAN units within 6" of this model.'

ABILITIES

The following abilities are common to several Craftworlds units:

Ancient Doom

You can re-roll failed hit rolls in the Fight phase for this unit in a turn in which it charges or is charged by a SLAANESH unit. However, you must add 1 to Morale tests for this unit if it is within 3" of any SLAANESH units.

Battle Focus

This unit can shoot in the Shooting phase as if it hasn't moved or Advanced (with the exception of Heavy weapons).

RUNES OF BATTLE AND RUNES OF FATE DISCIPLINES

Before the battle, generate the psychic powers for PSYKERS that can use powers from the Runes of Battle and Runes of Fate disciplines using the tables below. You can either roll a D3 to generate their powers randomly (re-roll any duplicate results), or you can select the psychic powers you wish the psyker to have.

Note that the Runes of Battle psychic powers have two names, and two effects. Each effect counts as a different psychic power, so in matched play games a Warlock Conclave that manifests *Conceal* could also attempt to manifest *Reveal*.

RUNES OF BATTLE DISCIPLINE

D3	PSYCHIC POWER
1	**Conceal/Reveal** *Conceal/Reveal* has a warp charge value of 6. If manifested, choose one of the following: *Conceal:* Your opponent must subtract 1 from all hit rolls for ranged weapons that target the psyker or friendly **ASURYANI INFANTRY** or **ASURYANI BIKER** units within 3" of the psyker until your next Psychic phase. *Reveal:* Choose an enemy unit within 18" of the psyker – it does not gain any bonus to its saving throws for being in cover until your next Psychic phase.
2	**Embolden/Horrify** *Embolden/Horrify* has a warp charge value of 6. If manifested, choose one of the following: *Embolden:* Add 2 to the Leadership characteristics of friendly **ASURYANI INFANTRY** or **ASURYANI BIKER** units within 3" of the psyker until your next Psychic phase. *Horrify:* Choose an enemy unit within 18" of the psyker – your opponent must subtract 1 from the Leadership of that unit takes until your next Psychic phase.
3	**Enhance/Drain** *Enhance/Drain* has a warp charge value of 7. If manifested, choose one of the following: *Enhance:* Add 1 to hit rolls in the Fight phase for friendly **ASURYANI INFANTRY** or **ASURYANI BIKER** units within 3" of the psyker until your next Psychic phase. *Drain:* Choose an enemy unit within 18" of the psyker – your opponent must subtract 1 from all hit rolls for that unit in the Fight phase until your next Psychic phase.

RUNES OF FATE DISCIPLINE
D3 PSYCHIC POWER

1

Guide

Guide has a warp charge value of 7. If manifested, choose a friendly **ASURYANI** unit within 24" of the psyker. You can re-roll failed hit rolls for that unit's ranged weapons until your next Psychic phase.

2

Doom

Doom has a warp charge value of 7. If manifested, choose an enemy unit within 24" of the psyker. You can re-roll failed wound rolls against that unit until your next Psychic phase.

3

Fortune

Fortune has a warp charge value of 7. If manifested, choose a friendly **ASURYANI** unit within 24" of the psyker. Until your next Psychic phase, whenever that unit suffers a wound, roll a D6. On a 5+ that wound is ignored. If a unit already has an ability with a similar effect (e.g. the Avatar of Khaine's Molten Body ability) this psychic power does not affect them.

WARGEAR

Many of the units you will find on the following pages reference one or more of the following wargear lists (e.g. Heavy Weapons). When this is the case, the unit may take any item from the appropriate list below. The profiles for the items in these lists can be found in the appendix (pg 114-117).

AUTARCH WEAPONS
- Avenger shuriken catapult
- Death spinner
- Fusion gun [1]
- Lasblaster [1]
- Power sword
- Reaper launcher [1]
- Scorpion chainsword

[1] *A model can only carry one of these weapons.*

HEAVY WEAPONS
- Aeldari missile launcher
- Bright lance
- Scatter laser
- Shuriken cannon
- Starcannon

VEHICLE EQUIPMENT
- Crystal targeting matrix
- Spirit stones
- Star engines
- Vectored engines

ELDRAD ULTHRAN

9 POWER

NAME	M	WS	BS	S	T	W	A	Ld	Sv
Eldrad Ulthran	7"	2+	2+	3	4	6	2	9	6+

Eldrad Ulthran is a single model armed with a shuriken pistol, a witchblade and the Staff of Ulthamar. Only one of this model may be included in your army.

WEAPON	RANGE	TYPE	S	AP	D	ABILITIES
Shuriken pistol	12"	Pistol 1	4	0	1	Each time you make a wound roll of 6+ for this weapon, that hit is resolved with an AP of -3 instead of 0.
Staff of Ulthamar	Melee	Melee	+2	-2	D3	-
Witchblade	Melee	Melee	User	0	D3	This weapon always wounds on a roll of 2+.

ABILITIES	**Ancient Doom, Battle Focus** (pg 10)	**Runes of the Farseer:** Once in each Psychic phase, you can re-roll any number of dice used for Eldrad Ulthran's attempt to manifest or deny a psychic power.
	Ghosthelm: Roll a D6 whenever Eldrad Ulthran suffers a mortal wound. On a roll of 5+, that wound is ignored.	**Spiritlink:** Whenever you pass a Psychic test for Eldrad Ulthran, you can add 1 to the next Psychic test you take for him until the end of the phase.
	Armour of the Last Runes: Eldrad Ulthran has a 3+ invulnerable save.	
PSYKER	Eldrad Ulthran can attempt to manifest three psychic powers in each friendly Psychic phase, and attempt to deny two psychic powers in each enemy Psychic phase. He knows the *Smite* power and three psychic powers from the Runes of Fate discipline (pg 11).	
FACTION KEYWORDS	AELDARI, ASURYANI, WARHOST, ULTHWÉ	
KEYWORDS	CHARACTER, INFANTRY, PSYKER, ELDRAD ULTHRAN	

PRINCE YRIEL

5 POWER

NAME	M	WS	BS	S	T	W	A	Ld	Sv
Prince Yriel	7"	2+	2+	3	3	6	4	9	3+

Prince Yriel is a single model armed with the Eye of Wrath, the Spear of Twilight and sunburst grenades. Only one of this model may be included in your army.

WEAPON	RANGE	TYPE	S	AP	D	ABILITIES
The Eye of Wrath	3"	Pistol D6	6	-2	1	This weapon can only be fired once per battle.
The Spear of Twilight	Melee	Melee	User	-2	D3	This weapon always wounds on a roll of 2+.
Sunburst grenade	6"	Grenade D6	4	-1	1	-

ABILITIES	**Ancient Doom, Battle Focus** (pg 10)	**Forceshield:** Prince Yriel has a 4+ invulnerable save.
	Cursed: You must re-roll saving throws of 6 for Prince Yriel in the Fight phase.	**The Path of Command:** You can re-roll hit rolls of 1 for friendly IYANDEN units within 6".
FACTION KEYWORDS	AELDARI, ASURYANI, WARHOST, IYANDEN	
KEYWORDS	CHARACTER, INFANTRY, PRINCE YRIEL	

4 POWER — ILLIC NIGHTSPEAR

NAME	M	WS	BS	S	T	W	A	Ld	Sv
Illic Nightspear	7"	2+	2+	3	3	5	4	9	5+

Illic Nightspear is a single model armed with Voidbringer, a shuriken pistol and a power sword. Only one of this model may be included in your army.

WEAPON	RANGE	TYPE	S	AP	D	ABILITIES
Shuriken pistol	12"	Pistol 1	4	0	1	Each time you make a wound roll of 6+ for this weapon, that hit is resolved with an AP of -3 instead of 0.
Voidbringer	48"	Heavy 1	4	-3	D3	This weapon can target an enemy **CHARACTER** even if they are not the closest enemy unit. This weapon wounds on a 2+, unless it is targeting a **VEHICLE**. Each time you roll a wound roll of 6+ for this weapon, it inflicts a mortal wound in addition to any other damage.
Power sword	Melee	Melee	User	-3	1	-

ABILITIES	Ancient Doom, Battle Focus (pg 10) **Appear Unbidden:** During deployment, you can set up Illic Nightspear walking the winding paths of the webway instead of placing him on the battlefield. At the beginning of the first battle round but before the first turn begins Illic Nightspear emerges from the webway – set him up anywhere on the battlefield that is more than 9" away from any enemy models.	**Bringer of the True Death:** You can re-roll hit and wounds rolls of 1 for Illic Nightspear's attacks when they target a **NECRON** unit. **Hunter Unseen:** Your opponent must subtract 1 from their hit rolls for attacks that target this unit. In addition, add 2 to this model's saving throws for being in cover instead of 1.

FACTION KEYWORDS	**AELDARI, ASURYANI, WARHOST, ALAITOC**
KEYWORDS	**CHARACTER, INFANTRY, ILLIC NIGHTSPEAR**

9 POWER — ASURMEN

NAME	M	WS	BS	S	T	W	A	Ld	Sv
Asurmen	7"	2+	2+	4	4	6	5	9	2+

Asurmen is a single model armed with the Sword of Asur and two avenger shuriken catapults. Only one of this model may be included in your army.

WEAPON	RANGE	TYPE	S	AP	D	ABILITIES
Avenger shuriken catapult	18"	Assault 2	4	0	1	Each time you make a wound roll of 6+ for this weapon, that hit is resolved with an AP of -3 instead of 0.
The Sword of Asur	Melee	Melee	+1	-3	D3	Each time you make a wound roll of 6+ for this weapon, the target suffers D3 mortal wounds in addition to any other damage.

ABILITIES	Ancient Doom, Battle Focus (pg 10) **Shield of Grace:** Asurmen has a 4+ invulnerable save against ranged weapons and a 3+ invulnerable save against melee weapons.	**Defence Tactics:** When Asurmen fires Overwatch, he hits on rolls of 5+, regardless of any modifiers. **Hand of Asuryan:** Friendly **ASPECT WARRIOR** units within 6" have a 5+ invulnerable save. Friendly Dire Avengers units have a 4+ invulnerable save instead.

FACTION KEYWORDS	**AELDARI, ASURYANI, ASPECT WARRIOR**
KEYWORDS	**CHARACTER, INFANTRY, PHOENIX LORD, ASURMEN**

JAIN ZAR

7 POWER

NAME	M	WS	BS	S	T	W	A	Ld	Sv
Jain Zar	8"	2+	2+	4	4	6	4	9	2+

Jain Zar is a single model armed with the Silent Death and the Blade of Destruction. Only one of this model may be included in your army.

WEAPON	RANGE	TYPE	S	AP	D	ABILITIES
Silent Death	12"	Assault 4	User	-3	1	-
Blade of Destruction	Melee	Melee	User	-3	D3	You can re-roll failed wound rolls for this weapon.

ABILITIES	
Ancient Doom, Battle Focus (pg 10) **Acrobatic:** Add 3 to your rolls when Jain Zar Advances or charges. **Disarming Strike:** At the beginning of each Fight phase you can choose a weapon on an enemy **Infantry** model within 1" of Jain Zar, and roll a D6. On a 3+ that model cannot use that weapon during this Fight phase.	**Banshee Mask:** Jain Zar always fights first in the Fight phase, even if she didn't charge. If the enemy has units that have charged, or that have a similar ability, then alternate choosing units to fight with, starting with the player whose turn is taking place. **War Shout:** Your opponent must subtract 1 from hit rolls in the Fight phase for attacks that target Jain Zar. **Cry of War Unending:** Enemy units cannot fire Overwatch at Jain Zar or at friendly units of Howling Banshees within 6".

FACTION KEYWORDS	**Aeldari, Asuryani, Aspect Warrior**
KEYWORDS	**Character, Infantry, Phoenix Lord, Jain Zar**

KARANDRAS

9 POWER

NAME	M	WS	BS	S	T	W	A	Ld	Sv
Karandras	7"	2+	2+	4	4	6	4	9	2+

Karandras is a single model armed with a scorpion chainsword, a scorpion's claw and sunburst grenades. Only one of this model may be included in your army.

WEAPON	RANGE	TYPE	S	AP	D	ABILITIES
Scorpion's claw (shooting)	12"	Assault 2	4	0	1	Each time you make a wound roll of 6+ for this weapon, that hit is resolved with an AP of -3 instead of 0.
Scorpion chainsword	Melee	Melee	+1	0	1	-
Scorpion's claw (melee)	Melee	Melee	x2	-3	D3	When attacking with this weapon, you must subtract 1 from the hit roll.
Sunburst grenade	6"	Grenade D6	4	-1	1	-

ABILITIES	
Ancient Doom, Battle Focus (pg 10) **Master of Stealth:** During deployment, you can set up Karandras in the shadows instead of placing him on the battlefield. If you do so, at the end of any of your Movement phases Karandras can stalk from his hiding place. When he does so set him up anywhere on the battlefield that is more than 9" away from any enemy models. **Shadow Strike:** Add 1 to hit rolls for attacks for Karandras that target a unit in cover.	**The Scorpion's Bite:** At the beginning of each Fight phase, roll four D6 if this model is within 1" of an enemy **Infantry** unit. For each roll of 5 or 6, that unit suffers a mortal wound. If two or more **Infantry** units are within 1", choose one to target before rolling any dice. **Death by a Thousand Stings:** Each time you roll a hit roll of 6+ when making a close combat attack for Karandras, or a model from a friendly Striking Scorpions unit within 6" of him, that model can immediately make another close combat attack using the same weapon. These extra attacks cannot generate any additional attacks.

FACTION KEYWORDS	**Aeldari, Asuryani, Aspect Warrior**
KEYWORDS	**Character, Infantry, Phoenix Lord, Karandras**

FUEGAN

NAME	M	WS	BS	S	T	W	A	Ld	Sv
Fuegan	7"	2+	2+	5	4	6	4	9	2+

Fuegan is a single model armed with the Fire Axe, a firepike and melta bombs. Only one of this model may be included in your army.

WEAPON	RANGE	TYPE	S	AP	D	ABILITIES
Firepike	18"	Assault 1	8	-4	D6	If the target is within half range of this weapon, roll two dice when inflicting damage with it and discard the lowest result.
Fire Axe	Melee	Melee	User	-4	D3	-
Melta bomb	6"	Grenade 1	8	-4	D6	You can re-roll failed wound rolls for this weapon when targeting a **Vehicle**.

ABILITIES	Ancient Doom, Battle Focus (pg 10)	**Last to Fall:** Roll a D6 whenever Fuegan suffers a wound or mortal wound. On a 5+ that wound is ignored.
	Assured Destruction: You can re-roll wound rolls of 1 in the Shooting phase for attacks Fuegan makes that target **Monsters** or **Vehicles**.	**Unquenchable Resolve:** At the end of the first Fight phase in which Fuegan suffers one or more unsaved wounds, his Strength and Attacks characteristics increase by 2. These bonuses last for the rest of the game.
	Unflinching Focus: You can re-roll hit rolls of 1 for Fuegan's ranged weapons, and for those of friendly Fire Dragons units within 6".	

FACTION KEYWORDS	**Aeldari, Asuryani, Aspect Warrior**
KEYWORDS	**Character, Infantry, Phoenix Lord, Fuegan**

BAHARROTH

NAME	M	WS	BS	S	T	W	A	Ld	Sv
Baharroth	14"	2+	2+	4	4	6	4	9	2+

Baharroth is a single model armed with the Shining Blade and a hawk's talon. Only one of this model may be included in your army.

WEAPON	RANGE	TYPE	S	AP	D	ABILITIES
Hawk's talon	24"	Assault 4	5	0	1	-
The Shining Blade	Melee	Melee	User	-2	D3	If a unit suffers any unsaved wounds from this weapon, your opponent must subtract 1 from that unit's hit rolls until the end of the turn.

ABILITIES	Ancient Doom, Battle Focus (pg 10)	**Baharroth's Grenade Pack:** Baharroth can fire a spread of grenades as he flies over enemy units in his Movement phase. To do so, after Baharroth has moved, pick one enemy unit that he flew over. Then, roll one D6 for each model in the enemy unit (up to a maximum of 3 dice). Each time you roll a 4+, the target unit suffers 1 mortal wound.
	Cry of the Wind: During deployment, you can set up Baharroth in the skies instead of placing him on the battlefield. At the end of any of your Movement phases Baharroth can descend on Swooping Hawk wings – set him up anywhere on the battlefield that is more than 9" away from any enemy models.	
	Skyleap: At the beginning of your Movement phase, if Baharroth is not within 1" of an enemy model he can leap back into the skies. Remove him from the battlefield. He can return to the battlefield as described in the Cry of the Wind ability. He may not both skyleap and descend on Swooping Hawk wings in the same turn. If the battle ends while Baharroth is in the skies, he is considered to be slain.	**The Brilliant Sun:** You can add 1 to the Leadership of friendly **Aspect Warrior** units within 6" of Baharroth. Add 2 to the Leadership of friendly Swooping Hawks units instead. **Blazing Fury:** You can re-roll hit rolls of 1 for friendly Swooping Hawks units within 6" of Baharroth.

FACTION KEYWORDS	**Aeldari, Asuryani, Aspect Warrior**
KEYWORDS	**Character, Infantry, Jump Pack, Phoenix Lord, Fly, Baharroth**

MAUGAN RA

NAME	M	WS	BS	S	T	W	A	Ld	Sv
Maugan Ra	6"	2+	2+	4	4	6	4	9	2+

Maugan Ra is a single model armed with the Maugetar. Only one of this model may be included in your army.

WEAPON	RANGE	TYPE	S	AP	D	ABILITIES
The Maugetar (shooting)	When attacking with this weapon, choose one of the profiles below. Each time you make a wound roll of 6+ for this weapon, that hit is resolved with an AP of -3 instead of -1.					
- Shrieker	36"	Assault 1	6	-1	1	If an INFANTRY model is slain by an attack made with this weapon, its unit suffers D3 mortal wounds.
- Shuriken	36"	Assault 4	6	-1	1	-
The Maugetar (scythe blade)	Melee	Melee	+2	-2	D3	-

| ABILITIES | Ancient Doom, Battle Focus (pg 10)

Whirlwind of Death: Maugan Ra can fire the Maugetar twice in each Shooting phase.

The Harvester: You can re-roll hit rolls of 1 for Maugan Ra's ranged weapon, and for those of friendly Dark Reapers units within 6". | **Inescapable Death:** Maugan Ra always hits on a 2+ when firing a ranged weapon, regardless of any modifiers (although he still only hits on rolls of 6 when firing Overwatch).

Legacy of Altansar: You can re-roll wound rolls of 1 for Maugan Ra's attacks that target CHAOS units. |
|---|---|---|

FACTION KEYWORDS	AELDARI, ASURYANI, ASPECT WARRIOR
KEYWORDS	CHARACTER, INFANTRY, PHOENIX LORD, MAUGAN RA

AUTARCH

NAME	M	WS	BS	S	T	W	A	Ld	Sv
Autarch	7"	2+	2+	3	3	5	4	9	3+

An Autarch is a single model armed with a shuriken pistol and sunburst grenades.

WEAPON	RANGE	TYPE	S	AP	D	ABILITIES
Fusion pistol	6"	Pistol 1	8	-4	D6	If the target is within half range of this weapon, roll two dice when inflicting damage with it and discard the lowest result.
Shuriken pistol	12"	Pistol 1	4	0	1	Each time you make a wound roll of 6+ for this weapon, that hit is resolved with an AP of -3 instead of 0.
Sunburst grenade	6"	Grenade D6	4	-1	1	-

WARGEAR OPTIONS	• This model may take either a banshee mask or mandiblasters. • This model may replace its shuriken pistol with a fusion pistol. • This model may take up to two weapons from the *Autarch Weapons* list.

| ABILITIES | Ancient Doom, Battle Focus (pg 10)

Banshee Mask: A model with a banshee mask always fights first in the Fight phase, even if it didn't charge. If the enemy has units that have charged, or that have a similar ability, then alternate choosing units to fight with, starting with the player whose turn is taking place.

Forceshield: This model has a 4+ invulnerable save. | **The Path of Command:** You can re-roll hit rolls of 1 for friendly <CRAFTWORLD> units within 6" of this model.

Mandiblasters: If this model has mandiblasters, at the beginning of each Fight phase, roll a D6 if this model is within 1" of an enemy INFANTRY unit. On a roll of 6, that unit suffers a mortal wound. If two or more INFANTRY units are within 1", choose one to target before rolling any dice. |
|---|---|

FACTION KEYWORDS	AELDARI, ASURYANI, WARHOST, <CRAFTWORLD>
KEYWORDS	CHARACTER, INFANTRY, AUTARCH

AUTARCH
with Swooping Hawk Wings

NAME	M	WS	BS	S	T	W	A	Ld	Sv
Autarch with Swooping Hawk Wings	14"	2+	2+	3	3	5	4	9	3+

An Autarch with Swooping Hawk wings is a single model armed with a shuriken pistol and sunburst grenades.

WEAPON	RANGE	TYPE	S	AP	D	ABILITIES
Fusion pistol	6"	Pistol 1	8	-4	D6	If the target is within half range of this weapon, roll two dice when inflicting damage with it and discard the lowest result.
Shuriken pistol	12"	Pistol 1	4	0	1	Each time you make a wound roll of 6+ for this weapon, that hit is resolved with an AP of -3 instead of 0.
Sunburst grenade	6"	Grenade D6	4	-1	1	-

WARGEAR OPTIONS	
	• This model may take either a banshee mask or mandiblasters. • This model may replace its shuriken pistol with a fusion pistol. • This model may take up to two weapons from the *Autarch Weapons* list.

ABILITIES		
	Ancient Doom, Battle Focus (pg 10)	**Forceshield:** This model has a 4+ invulnerable save.
	Children of Baharroth: During deployment, you can set up this model in the skies instead of placing it on the battlefield. At the end of any of your Movement phases this model can descend – set it up anywhere on the battlefield that is more than 9" away from any enemy models.	**Mandiblasters:** If this model has mandiblasters, at the beginning of each Fight phase, roll a D6 if this model is within 1" of an enemy **INFANTRY** unit. On a roll of 6, that unit suffers a mortal wound. If two or more **INFANTRY** units are within 1", choose one to target before rolling any dice.
	Banshee Mask: A model with a banshee mask always fights first in the Fight phase, even if it didn't charge. If the enemy has units that have charged, or that have a similar ability, then alternate choosing units to fight with, starting with the player whose turn is taking place.	**Skyleap:** At the beginning of your Movement phase, if this model is not within 1" of an enemy model it can leap back into the skies. Remove this model from the battlefield. It can return to the battlefield as described in the Children of Baharroth ability. This model may not both skyleap and descend on Swooping Hawk wings in the same turn. If the battle ends while this model is in the skies, it is considered to be slain.
	The Path of Command: You can re-roll hit rolls of 1 for friendly **<CRAFTWORLD>** units within 6" of this model.	

FACTION KEYWORDS	**AELDARI, ASURYANI, WARHOST, <CRAFTWORLD>**
KEYWORDS	**CHARACTER, INFANTRY, JUMP PACK, FLY, AUTARCH**

An Autarch of Craftworld Saim-Hann leaps into battle upon mighty pinions.

AUTARCH
WITH WARP JUMP GENERATOR

NAME	M	WS	BS	S	T	W	A	Ld	Sv
Autarch with Warp Jump Generator	7"	2+	2+	3	3	5	4	9	3+

An Autarch with warp jump generator is a single model armed with a shuriken pistol and sunburst grenades.

WEAPON	RANGE	TYPE	S	AP	D	ABILITIES
Fusion pistol	6"	Pistol 1	8	-4	D6	If the target is within half range of this weapon, roll two dice when inflicting damage with it and discard the lowest result.
Shuriken pistol	12"	Pistol 1	4	0	1	Each time you make a wound roll of 6+ for this weapon, that hit is resolved with an AP of -3 instead of 0.
Sunburst grenade	6"	Grenade D6	4	-1	1	-

WARGEAR OPTIONS	
	• This model may take either a banshee mask or mandiblasters.
	• This model may replace its shuriken pistol with a fusion pistol.
	• This model may take up to two weapons from the *Autarch Weapons* list.

ABILITIES	
	Ancient Doom, Battle Focus (pg 10)

Warp Jump Generator: When this model moves in the Movement phase, it can do so normally or using its warp jump generator. If it uses its warp jump generator it cannot Advance or charge this turn, but its Move characteristic is increased by 4D6" and it can **FLY** until the end of the phase.

Forceshield: This model has a 4+ invulnerable save.

The Path of Command: You can re-roll hit rolls of 1 for friendly <**CRAFTWORLD**> units within 6" of this model.

Mandiblasters: If this model has mandiblasters, at the beginning of each Fight phase, roll a D6 if this model is within 1" of an enemy **INFANTRY** unit. On a roll of 6, that unit suffers a mortal wound. If two or more **INFANTRY** units are within 1", choose one to target before rolling any dice.

Banshee Mask: A model with a banshee mask always fights first in the Fight phase, even if it didn't charge. If the enemy has units that have charged, or that have a similar ability, then alternate choosing units to fight with, starting with the player whose turn is taking place.

FACTION KEYWORDS	**AELDARI, ASURYANI, WARHOST, <CRAFTWORLD>**
KEYWORDS	**CHARACTER, INFANTRY, JUMP PACK, AUTARCH**

AUTARCH SKYRUNNER

NAME	M	WS	BS	S	T	W	A	Ld	Sv
Autarch Skyrunner	16"	2+	2+	3	4	6	4	9	3+

An Autarch Skyrunner is a single model armed with a shuriken pistol. Their Aeldari jetbike is equipped with a twin shuriken catapult.

WEAPON	RANGE	TYPE	S	AP	D	ABILITIES
Fusion pistol	6"	Pistol 1	8	-4	D6	If the target is within half range of this weapon, roll two dice when inflicting damage with it and discard the lowest result.
Laser lance (shooting)	6"	Assault 1	6	-4	2	-
Shuriken pistol	12"	Pistol 1	4	0	1	Each time you make a wound roll of 6+ for this weapon, that hit is resolved with an AP of -3 instead of 0.
Twin shuriken catapult	12"	Assault 4	4	0	1	Each time you make a wound roll of 6+ for this weapon, that hit is resolved with an AP of -3 instead of 0.
Laser lance (melee)	Melee	Melee	User	-4	2	If the bearer charged this turn, attacks with this weapon are made at Strength 6.

WARGEAR OPTIONS
- This model may take either a banshee mask or mandiblasters.
- This model may replace its shuriken pistol with a fusion pistol.
- This model may take up to two weapons from the *Autarch Weapons* list, or a laser lance and up to one weapon from the *Autarch Weapons* list.

ABILITIES

Ancient Doom, Battle Focus (pg 10)

Mandiblasters: If this model has mandiblasters, at the beginning of each Fight phase, roll a D6 if this model is within 1" of an enemy **INFANTRY** unit. On a roll of 6, that unit suffers a mortal wound. If two or more **INFANTRY** units are within 1", choose one to target before rolling any dice.

The Path of Command: You can re-roll hit rolls of 1 for friendly <CRAFTWORLD> units within 6" of this model.

Forceshield: This model has a 4+ invulnerable save.

Ride the Wind: When this model Advances, add 6" to its Move characteristic for that Movement phase instead of rolling a dice.

Banshee Mask: A model with a banshee mask always fights first in the Fight phase, even if it didn't charge. If the enemy has units that have charged, or that have a similar ability, then alternate choosing units to fight with, starting with the player whose turn is taking place.

FACTION KEYWORDS | AELDARI, ASURYANI, WARHOST, <CRAFTWORLD>

KEYWORDS | BIKER, CHARACTER, FLY, AUTARCH

AVATAR OF KHAINE

NAME	M	WS	BS	S	T	W	A	Ld	Sv
Avatar of Khaine	7"	2+	2+	6	6	8	5	9	3+

The Avatar of Khaine is a single model armed with the Wailing Doom. Only one of this model may be included in your army.

WEAPON	RANGE	TYPE	S	AP	D	ABILITIES
The Wailing Doom (shooting)	12"	Assault 1	8	-4	D6	Roll two dice when inflicting damage with this weapon and discard the lowest result.
The Wailing Doom (melee)	Melee	Melee	+2	-4	D6	Roll two dice when inflicting damage with this weapon and discard the lowest result.

ABILITIES

Ancient Doom, Battle Focus (pg 10)

Molten Body: Roll a D6 whenever the Avatar of Khaine suffers a wound or mortal wound. On a 5+ that wound is ignored.

Khaine Awakened: Friendly **ASURYANI** units within 12" of the Avatar of Khaine do not take Morale tests, and you can re-roll failed charge rolls for these units.

Daemon: The Avatar of Khaine has a 5+ invulnerable save.

FACTION KEYWORDS | AELDARI, ASURYANI, ASPECT WARRIOR, <CRAFTWORLD>

KEYWORDS | CHARACTER, MONSTER, DAEMON, AVATAR OF KHAINE

FARSEER

6 POWER

NAME	M	WS	BS	S	T	W	A	Ld	Sv
Farseer	7"	2+	2+	3	3	5	2	9	6+

A Farseer is a single model armed with a shuriken pistol and a witchblade.

WEAPON	RANGE	TYPE	S	AP	D	ABILITIES
Shuriken pistol	12"	Pistol 1	4	0	1	Each time you make a wound roll of 6+ for this weapon, that hit is resolved with an AP of -3 instead of 0.
Singing spear (shooting)	12"	Assault 1	9	0	D3	This weapon always wounds on a roll of 2+.
Witchblade	Melee	Melee	User	0	D3	This weapon always wounds on a roll of 2+.
Singing spear (melee)	Melee	Melee	User	0	D3	This weapon always wounds on a roll of 2+.

WARGEAR OPTIONS
- This model may replace its witchblade with a singing spear.

ABILITIES

Ancient Doom, Battle Focus (pg 10)

Ghosthelm: Roll a D6 whenever this model suffers a mortal wound. On a roll of 5+, that wound is ignored.

Rune Armour: This model has a 4+ invulnerable save.

Runes of the Farseer: Once in each Psychic phase, you can re-roll any number of dice used for this model's attempt to manifest or deny a psychic power.

PSYKER

This model can attempt to manifest two psychic powers in each friendly Psychic phase, and attempt to deny two psychic powers in each enemy Psychic phase. It knows the *Smite* power and two psychic powers from the Runes of Fate discipline (pg 11).

FACTION KEYWORDS AELDARI, ASURYANI, WARHOST, <CRAFTWORLD>

KEYWORDS CHARACTER, INFANTRY, PSYKER, FARSEER

FARSEER SKYRUNNER

9 POWER

NAME	M	WS	BS	S	T	W	A	Ld	Sv
Farseer Skyrunner	16"	2+	2+	3	4	6	2	9	4+

A Farseer Skyrunner is a single model armed with a shuriken pistol and a witchblade. Their Aeldari jetbike is equipped with a twin shuriken catapult.

WEAPON	RANGE	TYPE	S	AP	D	ABILITIES
Shuriken pistol	12"	Pistol 1	4	0	1	Each time you make a wound roll of 6+ for this weapon, that hit is resolved with an AP of -3 instead of 0.
Singing spear (shooting)	12"	Assault 1	9	0	D3	This weapon always wounds on a roll of 2+.
Twin shuriken catapult	12"	Assault 4	4	0	1	Each time you make a wound roll of 6+ for this weapon, that hit is resolved with an AP of -3 instead of 0.
Singing spear (melee)	Melee	Melee	User	0	D3	This weapon always wounds on a roll of 2+.
Witchblade	Melee	Melee	User	0	D3	This weapon always wounds on a roll of 2+.

WARGEAR OPTIONS
- This model may replace its witchblade with a singing spear.

ABILITIES

Ancient Doom, Battle Focus (pg 10)

Ghosthelm: Roll a D6 whenever this model suffers a mortal wound. On a roll of 5+, that wound is ignored.

Rune armour: This model has a 4+ invulnerable save.

Runes of the Farseer: Once in each Psychic phase, you can re-roll any number of dice used for this model's attempt to manifest or deny a psychic power.

Ride the Wind: When this model Advances, add 6" to its Move characteristic for that Movement phase instead of rolling a dice.

PSYKER

This model can attempt to manifest two psychic powers in each friendly Psychic phase, and attempt to deny two psychic powers in each enemy Psychic phase. It knows the *Smite* power and two psychic powers from the Runes of Fate discipline (pg 11).

FACTION KEYWORDS AELDARI, ASURYANI, WARHOST, <CRAFTWORLD>

KEYWORDS BIKER, CHARACTER, FLY, PSYKER, FARSEER SKYRUNNER

WARLOCK CONCLAVE

6 POWER

NAME	M	WS	BS	S	T	W	A	Ld	Sv
Warlock	7"	3+	3+	3	3	2	2	8	6+

This unit contains 2 Warlocks. It can include up to 8 additional Warlocks (**Power Rating +3 per model**). Each model is armed with a shuriken pistol and a witchblade.

WEAPON	RANGE	TYPE	S	AP	D	ABILITIES
Singing spear (shooting)	12"	Assault 1	9	0	D3	This weapon always wounds on a roll of 2+.
Shuriken pistol	12"	Pistol 1	4	0	1	Each time you make a wound roll of 6+ for this weapon, that hit is resolved with an AP of -3 instead of 0.
Singing spear (melee)	Melee	Melee	User	0	D3	This weapon always wounds on a roll of 2+.
Witchblade	Melee	Melee	User	0	D3	This weapon always wounds on a roll of 2+.

WARGEAR OPTIONS	• Any model may replace its witchblade with a singing spear.

ABILITIES	**Ancient Doom, Battle Focus** (pg 10)	**Destructor:** When this unit manifests the *Smite* psychic power, it has a range of 9" rather than 18". In addition, if this unit consists of 1-3 models when it manifests *Smite*, it only deals a single mortal wound. If it consists of 7-10 models when it manifests *Smite*, it always deals D6 mortal wounds.
	Rune Armour: Models in this unit have a 4+ invulnerable save.	

PSYKER	If this unit has 1-3 models it can attempt to manifest one psychic power in each friendly Psychic phase, and attempt to deny one psychic power in each enemy Psychic phase. If this unit has 4-6 models it can attempt to manifest two powers and deny two powers, and if it has 7-10 models it can attempt to manifest three powers and deny three powers. This unit knows the *Smite* power and two psychic powers from the Runes of Battle discipline (pg 10).
	If this unit has more than one model, when manifesting or denying a psychic power, first select a model in the unit – measure range, visibility, etc. from this model. If this unit suffers Perils of the Warp, it suffers D3 mortal wounds as described in the core rules, but units within 6" will only suffer damage if the Perils of the Warp causes the last model in the manifesting unit to be slain.

FACTION KEYWORDS	AELDARI, ASURYANI, WARHOST, <CRAFTWORLD>
KEYWORDS	INFANTRY, PSYKER, WARLOCK CONCLAVE

WARLOCK

3 POWER

NAME	M	WS	BS	S	T	W	A	Ld	Sv
Warlock	7"	3+	3+	3	3	2	2	8	6+

A Warlock is a single model armed with a shuriken pistol and a witchblade.

WEAPON	RANGE	TYPE	S	AP	D	ABILITIES
Singing spear (shooting)	12"	Assault 1	9	0	D3	This weapon always wounds on a roll of 2+.
Shuriken pistol	12"	Pistol 1	4	0	1	Each time you make a wound roll of 6+ for this weapon, that hit is resolved with an AP of -3 instead of 0.
Singing spear (melee)	Melee	Melee	User	0	D3	This weapon always wounds on a roll of 2+.
Witchblade	Melee	Melee	User	0	D3	This weapon always wounds on a roll of 2+.

WARGEAR OPTIONS	• This model may replace its witchblade with a singing spear.

ABILITIES	**Ancient Doom, Battle Focus** (pg 10)	**Destructor:** When this model manifests the *Smite* psychic power, it has a range of 9" rather than 18" and only deals a single mortal wound.
	Rune Armour: This model has a 4+ invulnerable save.	

PSYKER	This model can attempt to manifest one psychic power in each friendly Psychic phase, and attempt to deny one psychic power in each enemy Psychic phase. It knows the *Smite* power and one psychic power from the Runes of Battle discipline (pg 10).

FACTION KEYWORDS	AELDARI, ASURYANI, WARHOST, <CRAFTWORLD>
KEYWORDS	CHARACTER, INFANTRY, PSYKER, WARLOCK

WARLOCK SKYRUNNER
CONCLAVE

NAME	M	WS	BS	S	T	W	A	Ld	Sv
Warlock Skyrunner	16"	3+	3+	3	4	3	2	8	4+

This unit contains 2 Warlock Skyrunners. It can include up to 8 additional Warlock Skyrunners (**Power Rating +5 per model**). Each model is armed with a shuriken pistol and a witchblade. Each of their Aeldari jetbikes is equipped with a twin shuriken catapult.

WEAPON	RANGE	TYPE	S	AP	D	ABILITIES
Singing spear (shooting)	12"	Assault 1	9	0	D3	This weapon always wounds on a roll of 2+.
Shuriken pistol	12"	Pistol 1	4	0	1	Each time you make a wound roll of 6+ for a shuriken weapon, that hit is resolved with an AP of -3 instead of 0.
Twin shuriken catapult	12"	Assault 4	4	0	1	
Singing spear (melee)	Melee	Melee	User	0	D3	This weapon always wounds on a roll of 2+.
Witchblade	Melee	Melee	User	0	D3	This weapon always wounds on a roll of 2+.

WARGEAR OPTIONS	• Any model may replace its witchblade with a singing spear.

ABILITIES	Ancient Doom, Battle Focus (pg 10) Rune Armour: Models in this unit have a 4+ invulnerable save. Ride the Wind: When this unit Advances, add 6" to its Move characteristic for that Movement phase instead of rolling a dice.	Destructor: When this unit manifests the *Smite* psychic power, it has a range of 9" rather than 18". In addition, if this unit consists of 1-3 models when it manifests *Smite*, it only deals a single mortal wound. If it consists of 7-10 models when it manifests *Smite*, it always deals D6 mortal wounds.
PSYKER	If this unit has 1-3 models it can attempt to manifest one psychic power in each friendly Psychic phase, and attempt to deny one psychic power in each enemy Psychic phase. If this unit has 4-6 models it can attempt to manifest two powers and deny two powers, and if it has 7-10 models it can attempt to manifest three powers and deny three powers. This unit knows the *Smite* power and two psychic powers from the Runes of Battle discipline (pg 10). If this unit consists of more than one model, when manifesting or denying a psychic power, first select a model in the unit – measure range, visibility, etc. from this model. If this unit suffers Perils of the Warp, it suffers D3 mortal wounds as described in the core rules, but units within 6" will only suffer damage if the Perils of the Warp causes the last model in the manifesting unit to be slain.	
FACTION KEYWORDS	**AELDARI, ASURYANI, WARHOST, <CRAFTWORLD>**	
KEYWORDS	**BIKER, FLY, PSYKER, WARLOCK SKYRUNNER CONCLAVE**	

WARLOCK SKYRUNNER

NAME	M	WS	BS	S	T	W	A	Ld	Sv
Warlock Skyrunner	16"	3+	3+	3	4	3	2	8	4+

A Warlock Skyrunner is a single model armed with a shuriken pistol and a witchblade. Its Aeldari jetbike is equipped with a twin shuriken catapult.

WEAPON	RANGE	TYPE	S	AP	D	ABILITIES
Singing spear (shooting)	12"	Assault 1	9	0	D3	This weapon always wounds on a roll of 2+.
Shuriken pistol	12"	Pistol 1	4	0	1	Each time you make a wound roll of 6+ for a shuriken weapon, that hit is resolved with an AP of -3 instead of 0.
Twin shuriken catapult	12"	Assault 4	4	0	1	
Singing spear (melee)	Melee	Melee	User	0	D3	This weapon always wounds on a roll of 2+.
Witchblade	Melee	Melee	User	0	D3	This weapon always wounds on a roll of 2+.

WARGEAR OPTIONS	• This model may replace its witchblade with a singing spear.

ABILITIES	Ancient Doom, Battle Focus (pg 10) Ride the Wind: When this model Advances, add 6" to its Move characteristic for that Movement phase instead of rolling a dice.	Rune Armour: This model has a 4+ invulnerable save. Destructor: When this model manifests the *Smite* psychic power, it has a range of 9" rather than 18" and only deals a single mortal wound.
PSYKER	This model can attempt to manifest one psychic power in each friendly Psychic phase, and attempt to deny one psychic power in each enemy Psychic phase. It knows the *Smite* power and one psychic power from the Runes of Battle discipline (pg 10).	
FACTION KEYWORDS	**AELDARI, ASURYANI, WARHOST, <CRAFTWORLD>**	
KEYWORDS	**BIKER, CHARACTER, FLY, PSYKER, WARLOCK SKYRUNNER**	

☠ ④ SPIRITSEER

NAME	M	WS	BS	S	T	W	A	Ld	Sv
Spiritseer	7"	2+	2+	3	3	4	2	8	6+

A Spiritseer is a single model armed with a shuriken pistol and a witch staff.

WEAPON	RANGE	TYPE	S	AP	D	ABILITIES
Shuriken pistol	12"	Pistol 1	4	0	1	Each time you make a wound roll of 6+ for this weapon, that hit is resolved with an AP of -3 instead of 0.
Witch staff	Melee	Melee	User	0	2	This weapon always wounds on a roll of 2+.

ABILITIES	Ancient Doom, Battle Focus (pg 10) Rune Armour: This model has a 4+ invulnerable save.	Spirit Mark: You can re-roll hit rolls of 1 for friendly <Craftworld> Spirit Host units' attacks against enemy units that are within 6" of this model.

PSYKER	This model can attempt to manifest one psychic power in each friendly Psychic phase, and attempt to deny one psychic power in each enemy Psychic phase. It knows the *Smite* power and one psychic power from the Runes of Battle discipline (pg 10).
FACTION KEYWORDS	AELDARI, ASURYANI, SPIRIT HOST, <CRAFTWORLD>
KEYWORDS	CHARACTER, INFANTRY, PSYKER, SPIRITSEER

▶ ④ GUARDIAN DEFENDERS

NAME	M	WS	BS	S	T	W	A	Ld	Sv
Guardian	7"	3+	3+	3	3	1	1	7	5+
Heavy Weapon Platform	7"	6+	3+	3	3	2	1	7	3+

This unit contains 10 Guardians. It can include up to 10 additional Guardians (**Power Rating +4**). For every 10 Guardians in the unit, you may include one Heavy Weapon Platform.
- Each Guardian is armed with a shuriken catapult and sunburst grenades.
- Each Heavy Weapon Platform is armed with a shuriken cannon.

WEAPON	RANGE	TYPE	S	AP	D	ABILITIES
Shuriken cannon	24"	Assault 3	6	0	1	Each time you make a wound roll of 6+ for this weapon, that hit is resolved with an AP of -3 instead of 0.
Shuriken catapult	12"	Assault 2	4	0	1	Each time you make a wound roll of 6+ for this weapon, that hit is resolved with an AP of -3 instead of 0.
Sunburst grenade	6"	Grenade D6	4	-1	1	-

WARGEAR OPTIONS	• Any Heavy Weapon Platform may replace its shuriken cannon with a weapon from the *Heavy Weapons* list.
ABILITIES	Ancient Doom, Battle Focus (pg 10) Crewed Weapon: A Heavy Weapon Platform can only fire its ranged weapon if a Guardian from its unit is within 3" and 'fires' it instead of shooting any of their own weapons. A single Guardian cannot operate multiple Heavy Weapon Platforms in this way in a single turn.
FACTION KEYWORDS	AELDARI, ASURYANI, WARHOST, <CRAFTWORLD>
KEYWORDS (GUARDIAN)	INFANTRY, GUARDIAN DEFENDERS
KEYWORDS (HEAVY WEAPON PLATFORM)	INFANTRY, ARTILLERY, HEAVY WEAPON PLATFORM

▶ ③ STORM GUARDIANS

NAME	M	WS	BS	S	T	W	A	Ld	Sv
Guardian	7"	3+	3+	3	3	1	1	7	5+

This unit contains 8 Guardians. It can include up to 8 additional Guardians (**Power Rating +3**) or up to 16 additional Guardians (**Power Rating +6**). Each model is armed with a shuriken pistol, an Aeldari blade and sunburst grenades.

WEAPON	RANGE	TYPE	S	AP	D	ABILITIES
Flamer	8"	Assault D6	4	0	1	This weapon automatically hits its target.
Fusion gun	12"	Assault 1	8	-4	D6	If the target is within half range of this weapon, roll two dice when inflicting damage with it and discard the lowest result.
Shuriken pistol	12"	Pistol 1	4	0	1	Each time you make a wound roll of 6+ for this weapon, that hit is resolved with an AP of -3 instead of 0.
Aeldari blade	Melee	Melee	User	0	1	You can re-roll failed hit rolls for this weapon.
Chainsword	Melee	Melee	User	0	1	Each time the bearer fights, it can make 1 additional attack with this weapon.
Power sword	Melee	Melee	User	-3	1	-
Sunburst grenade	6"	Grenade D6	4	-1	1	-

WARGEAR OPTIONS	• Up to two Guardians may replace their shuriken pistol and Aeldari blade with either a flamer or a fusion gun. • Up to two Guardians may replace their Aeldari blade with a power sword. • Any Guardian may replace their Aeldari blade with a chainsword.
ABILITIES	Ancient Doom, Battle Focus (pg 10)
FACTION KEYWORDS	AELDARI, ASURYANI, WARHOST, <CRAFTWORLD>
KEYWORDS	INFANTRY, STORM GUARDIANS

⚡ ⑤ WINDRIDERS

NAME	M	WS	BS	S	T	W	A	Ld	Sv
Windrider	16"	3+	3+	3	4	2	1	7	4+

This unit contains 3 Windriders. It can include up to 3 additional Windriders (**Power Rating +5**) or up to 6 additional Windriders (**Power Rating +10**). Each of their Aeldari jetbikes is equipped with a twin shuriken catapult.

WEAPON	RANGE	TYPE	S	AP	D	ABILITIES
Scatter laser	36"	Heavy 4	6	0	1	-
Shuriken cannon	24"	Assault 3	6	0	1	Each time you make a wound roll of 6+ for this weapon, that hit is resolved with an AP of -3 instead of 0.
Twin shuriken catapult	12"	Assault 4	4	0	1	Each time you make a wound roll of 6+ for this weapon, that hit is resolved with an AP of -3 instead of 0.

WARGEAR OPTIONS	• Any Aeldari jetbike may replace its twin shuriken catapult with either a scatter laser or a shuriken cannon.	
ABILITIES	Ancient Doom, Battle Focus (pg 10)	**Ride the Wind:** When this unit Advances, add 6" to its Move characteristic for that Movement phase instead of rolling a dice.
FACTION KEYWORDS	AELDARI, ASURYANI, WARHOST, <CRAFTWORLD>	
KEYWORDS	BIKER, FLY, WINDRIDERS	

RANGERS

5 POWER

NAME	M	WS	BS	S	T	W	A	Ld	Sv
Ranger	7"	3+	3+	3	3	1	1	7	5+

This unit contains 5 Rangers. It can include up to 5 additional Rangers (**Power Rating +5**). Each model is armed with a shuriken pistol and a ranger long rifle.

WEAPON	RANGE	TYPE	S	AP	D	ABILITIES
Shuriken pistol	12"	Pistol 1	4	0	1	Each time you make a wound roll of 6+ for this weapon, that hit is resolved with an AP of -3 instead of 0.
Ranger long rifle	36"	Heavy 1	4	0	1	This weapon may target a **CHARACTER** even if it is not the closest enemy unit. Each time you roll a wound roll of 6+ for this weapon, it inflicts a mortal wound in addition to any other damage.

ABILITIES	Ancient Doom, Battle Focus (pg 10)	**Appear Unbidden:** During deployment, you can set up a unit of Rangers walking the winding paths of the webway instead of placing it on the battlefield. At the beginning of the first battle round but before the first turn begins the unit of Rangers emerge from the webway – set them up anywhere on the battlefield that is more than 9" away from any enemy models.
	Cameleoline Cloaks: Your opponent must subtract 1 from their hit rolls for attacks that target this unit. In addition, add 2 to saving throws made for models from this unit that are in cover, instead of 1.	

FACTION KEYWORDS	AELDARI, ASURYANI, WARHOST, <CRAFTWORLD>
KEYWORDS	INFANTRY, RANGERS

DIRE AVENGERS

3 POWER

NAME	M	WS	BS	S	T	W	A	Ld	Sv
Dire Avenger	7"	3+	3+	3	3	1	1	8	4+
Dire Avenger Exarch	7"	3+	3+	3	3	2	2	8	4+

This unit contains 5 Dire Avengers. It can include up to 5 additional Dire Avengers (**Power Rating +3**). A Dire Avenger Exarch can take the place of one Dire Avenger. Each model is armed with an avenger shuriken catapult and sunburst grenades.

WEAPON	RANGE	TYPE	S	AP	D	ABILITIES
Avenger shuriken catapult	18"	Assault 2	4	0	1	Each time you make a wound roll of 6+ for this weapon, that hit is resolved with an AP of -3 instead of 0.
Shuriken pistol	12"	Pistol 1	4	0	1	Each time you make a wound roll of 6+ for this weapon, that hit is resolved with an AP of -3 instead of 0.
Diresword	Melee	Melee	User	-2	1	Each time you make a wound roll of 6+ for this weapon, the target suffers a mortal wound in addition to any other damage.
Power glaive	Melee	Melee	+1	-2	1	-
Sunburst grenade	6"	Grenade D6	4	-1	1	-

WARGEAR OPTIONS	• The Dire Avenger Exarch may replace their avenger shuriken catapult with one of the following: - Two avenger shuriken catapults - Shuriken pistol and power glaive - Shuriken pistol and diresword - Shimmershield and power glaive

ABILITIES	Ancient Doom, Battle Focus (pg 10)	**Defence Tactics:** When this unit shoots Overwatch, it hits on rolls of 5+, regardless of any modifiers.
	Battle Fortune: The Dire Avenger Exarch has a 4+ invulnerable save.	**Shimmershield:** A unit which includes a model with a shimmershield has a 5+ invulnerable save.

FACTION KEYWORDS	AELDARI, ASURYANI, ASPECT WARRIOR, <CRAFTWORLD>
KEYWORDS	INFANTRY, DIRE AVENGERS

HOWLING BANSHEES

NAME	M	WS	BS	S	T	W	A	Ld	Sv
Howling Banshee	8"	3+	3+	3	3	1	2	8	4+
Howling Banshee Exarch	8"	3+	3+	3	3	2	3	8	4+

This unit contains 5 Howling Banshees. It can include up to 5 additional Howling Banshees (**Power Rating +4**). A Howling Banshee Exarch can take the place of one Howling Banshee. Each model is armed with a shuriken pistol and a power sword.

WEAPON	RANGE	TYPE	S	AP	D	ABILITIES
Shuriken pistol	12"	Pistol 1	4	0	1	Each time you make a wound roll of 6+ for this weapon, that hit is resolved with an AP of -3 instead of 0.
Triskele (shooting)	12"	Assault 3	3	-2	1	-
Executioner	Melee	Melee	+2	-3	D3	When attacking with this weapon, you must subtract 1 from the hit roll.
Mirrorswords	Melee	Melee	User	-2	1	You can re-roll failed hit rolls in the Fight phase for this weapon.
Power sword	Melee	Melee	User	-3	1	-
Triskele (melee)	Melee	Melee	User	-2	1	-

WARGEAR OPTIONS	• The Howling Banshee Exarch may replace her power sword with a triskele or an executioner. • The Howling Banshee Exarch may replace her shuriken pistol and power sword with mirrorswords.

ABILITIES	Ancient Doom, Battle Focus (pg 10) **Banshee Mask:** Models in this unit always fight first in the Fight phase, even if they didn't charge. If the enemy has units that have charged, or that have a similar ability, then alternate choosing units to fight with, starting with the player whose turn is taking place.	**Acrobatic:** Add 3 to your rolls when this unit Advances or charges. **War Shout:** Your opponent must subtract 1 from hit rolls in the Fight phase for attacks that target a unit that includes a Howling Banshee Exarch.

FACTION KEYWORDS	Aeldari, Asuryani, Aspect Warrior, <Craftworld>
KEYWORDS	Infantry, Howling Banshees

Swift as the wind, the Howling Banshees sprint into battle with nerve-shredding screams.

STRIKING SCORPIONS

NAME	M	WS	BS	S	T	W	A	Ld	Sv
Striking Scorpion	7"	3+	3+	3	3	1	2	8	3+
Striking Scorpion Exarch	7"	3+	3+	3	3	2	3	8	3+

This unit contains 5 Striking Scorpions. It can include up to 5 additional Striking Scorpions (**Power Rating +5**). A Striking Scorpion Exarch can take the place of one Striking Scorpion. Each model is armed with a shuriken pistol, a scorpion chainsword and sunburst grenades.

WEAPON	RANGE	TYPE	S	AP	D	ABILITIES
Chainsabres (shooting)	12"	Pistol 2	4	0	1	Each time you make a wound roll of 6+ for this weapon, that hit is resolved with an AP of -3 instead of 0.
Scorpion's claw (shooting)	12"	Assault 2	4	0	1	Each time you make a wound roll of 6+ for this weapon, that hit is resolved with an AP of -3 instead of 0.
Shuriken pistol	12"	Pistol 1	4	0	1	Each time you make a wound roll of 6+ for this weapon, that hit is resolved with an AP of -3 instead of 0.
Biting blade	Melee	Melee	+2	-1	2	-
Chainsabres (melee)	Melee	Melee	+1	0	1	Each time the bearer fights, it can make 1 additional attack with this weapon.
Scorpion chainsword	Melee	Melee	+1	0	1	-
Scorpion's claw (melee)	Melee	Melee	x2	-3	D3	When attacking with this weapon, you must subtract 1 from the hit roll.
Sunburst grenade	6"	Grenade D6	4	-1	1	-

WARGEAR OPTIONS	
	• The Striking Scorpion Exarch may replace their shuriken pistol with a scorpion's claw.
	• The Striking Scorpion Exarch may replace their scorpion chainsword with a biting blade.
	• The Striking Scorpion Exarch may replace their shuriken pistol and scorpion chainsword with chainsabres.

ABILITIES	
	Ancient Doom, Battle Focus (pg 10)

Masters of Stealth: During deployment, you can set up a unit of Striking Scorpions in the shadows instead of placing it on the battlefield. If you do so, at the end of any of your Movement phase the Striking Scorpions can stalk from their hiding place. When they do so set them up anywhere on the battlefield that is more than 9" away from any enemy models.

Shadow Strike: Add 1 to hit rolls for attacks for this unit that target a unit in cover.

Mandiblasters: At the beginning of each Fight phase, roll a D6 for each model in this unit if the unit is within 1" of an enemy **INFANTRY** unit. For each roll of 6, that unit suffers a mortal wound. If two or more **INFANTRY** units are within 1", choose one to target before rolling any dice.

Sustained Attack: Each time you roll a hit roll of 6+ when making a close combat attack for a Striking Scorpion Exarch, that model can immediately make another close combat attack using the same weapon. These extra attacks cannot generate any additional attacks.

FACTION KEYWORDS	**AELDARI, ASURYANI, ASPECT WARRIOR, <CRAFTWORLD>**
KEYWORDS	**INFANTRY, STRIKING SCORPIONS**

Striking Scorpions advance through the shadows to strike with unstoppable force.

6 POWER   FIRE DRAGONS

NAME	M	WS	BS	S	T	W	A	Ld	Sv
Fire Dragon	7"	3+	3+	3	3	1	1	8	3+
Fire Dragon Exarch	7"	3+	3+	3	3	2	2	8	3+

This unit contains 5 Fire Dragons. It can include up to 5 additional Fire Dragons (**Power Rating +6**). A Fire Dragon Exarch can take the place of one Fire Dragon. Each model is armed with a fusion gun and melta bombs.

WEAPON	RANGE	TYPE	S	AP	D	ABILITIES
Dragon's breath flamer	8"	Assault D6	5	-1	1	This weapon automatically hits its target.
Firepike	18"	Assault 1	8	-4	D6	If the target is within half range of this weapon, roll two dice when inflicting damage with it and discard the lowest result.
Fusion gun	12"	Assault 1	8	-4	D6	If the target is within half range of this weapon, roll two dice when inflicting damage with it and discard the lowest result.
Melta bomb	6"	Grenade 1	8	-4	D6	You can re-roll failed wound rolls for this weapon when targeting a **VEHICLE**.

WARGEAR OPTIONS	The Fire Dragon Exarch may replace their fusion gun with a dragon's breath flamer or a firepike.
ABILITIES	Ancient Doom, Battle Focus (pg 10) **Crack Shot:** You can re-roll hit rolls of 1 for a Fire Dragon Exarch's ranged weapons.	**Assured Destruction:** You can re-roll wound rolls of 1 in the Shooting phase for attacks this unit make that target **MONSTERS** or **VEHICLES**.
FACTION KEYWORDS	AELDARI, ASURYANI, ASPECT WARRIOR, <CRAFTWORLD>
KEYWORDS	INFANTRY, FIRE DRAGONS

10 POWER   WRAITHGUARD

NAME	M	WS	BS	S	T	W	A	Ld	Sv
Wraithguard	5"	3+	3+	5	5	3	1	9	3+

This unit contains 5 Wraithguard. It can include up to 5 additional Wraithguard (**Power Rating +10**). Each model is armed with a wraithcannon and Wraithguard fists.

WEAPON	RANGE	TYPE	S	AP	D	ABILITIES
D-scythe	8"	Assault D3	10	-4	1	When a unit fires its D-scythes, roll once for the number of attacks and use this for all D-scythes fired by the unit in this phase. This weapon automatically hits its target.
Wraithcannon	12"	Assault 1	10	-4	D6	-
Wraithguard fists	Melee	Melee	User	-1	D3	-

WARGEAR OPTIONS	• The entire unit may replace their wraithcannons with D-scythes.
ABILITIES	Ancient Doom (pg 10) **Implacable:** This unit can Fall Back and still shoot in a turn that it does so.
FACTION KEYWORDS	AELDARI, ASURYANI, SPIRIT HOST, <CRAFTWORLD>
KEYWORDS	INFANTRY, WRAITHGUARD

(10) POWER — WRAITHBLADES

NAME	M	WS	BS	S	T	W	A	Ld	Sv
Wraithblade	5"	3+	3+	5	5	3	2	9	3+

This unit contains 5 Wraithblades. It can include up to 5 additional Wraithblades (**Power Rating +10**). Each model is armed with ghostswords.

WEAPON	RANGE	TYPE	S	AP	D	ABILITIES
Ghostaxe	Melee	Melee	+2	-3	D3	When attacking with this weapon, you must subtract 1 from the hit roll.
Ghostswords	Melee	Melee	+1	-2	1	Each time the bearer fights, it can make 1 additional attack with this weapon.

WARGEAR OPTIONS	• The entire unit may replace their ghostswords with ghostaxes and forceshields.

ABILITIES	Ancient Doom (pg 10) **Fires of Wrath:** Add 1 to the Attacks characteristic of models in this unit in a turn in which it charges.	**Forceshield:** A model equipped with a forceshield has a 4+ invulnerable save.

FACTION KEYWORDS	AELDARI, ASURYANI, SPIRIT HOST, <CRAFTWORLD>
KEYWORDS	INFANTRY, WRAITHBLADES

(9) POWER — WAVE SERPENT

DAMAGE
Some of this model's characteristics change as it suffers damage, as shown below:

REMAINING W	M	BS	A
7-13+	16"	3+	3
4-6	12"	4+	D3
1-3	8"	5+	1

NAME	M	WS	BS	S	T	W	A	Ld	Sv
Wave Serpent	*	6+	*	6	7	13	*	8	3+

A Wave Serpent is a single model equipped with a twin shuriken cannon and a twin shuriken catapult.

WEAPON	RANGE	TYPE	S	AP	D	ABILITIES
Shuriken cannon	24"	Assault 3	6	0	1	Each time you make a wound roll of 6+ for this weapon, that hit is resolved with an AP of -3 instead of 0.
Twin Aeldari missile launcher	When attacking with this weapon, choose one of the profiles below.					
- Sunburst missile	48"	Heavy 2D6	4	-1	1	-
- Starshot missile	48"	Heavy 2	8	-2	D6	-
Twin bright lance	36"	Heavy 2	8	-4	D6	-
Twin scatter laser	36"	Heavy 8	6	0	1	-
Twin shuriken cannon	24"	Assault 6	6	0	1	Each time you make a wound roll of 6+ for this weapon, that hit is resolved with an AP of -3 instead of 0.
Twin shuriken catapult	12"	Assault 4	4	0	1	Each time you make a wound roll of 6+ for this weapon, that hit is resolved with an AP of -3 instead of 0.
Twin starcannon	36"	Heavy 4	6	-3	3	-

WARGEAR OPTIONS	• This model may replace its twin shuriken cannon with a twin bright lance, a twin scatter laser, a twin starcannon or a twin Aeldari missile launcher. • This model may replace its twin shuriken catapult with a shuriken cannon. • This model may take items from the *Vehicle Equipment* list.

ABILITIES	**Serpent Shield:** Any damage suffered by a Wave Serpent from a ranged weapon is reduced by 1, to a minimum of 1. In addition, once per battle, a Wave Serpent can discharge its serpent shield. If it does so, roll a D6. On a 2+ the nearest visible enemy unit within 24" suffers D3 mortal wounds. The Wave Serpent then gains no benefit from this ability for the remainder of the battle.	**Explodes:** If this model is reduced to 0 wounds, roll a D6 before removing it from the battlefield and before any embarked models disembark. On a 6 it explodes, and each unit within 6" suffers D3 mortal wounds. **Hover Tank:** Distance and ranges are always measured to and from this model's hull, even though it has a base.

TRANSPORT:	A Wave Serpent can transport 12 PHOENIX LORD or <CRAFTWORLD> INFANTRY models, other than JUMP PACK models. Wraithguard and Wraithblades count as 2 models each.

FACTION KEYWORDS	AELDARI, ASURYANI, WARHOST, <CRAFTWORLD>
KEYWORDS	VEHICLE, TRANSPORT, FLY, WAVE SERPENT

SWOOPING HAWKS

NAME	M	WS	BS	S	T	W	A	Ld	Sv
Swooping Hawk	14"	3+	3+	3	3	1	1	8	4+
Swooping Hawk Exarch	14"	3+	3+	3	3	2	2	8	4+

This unit contains 5 Swooping Hawks. It can include up to 5 additional Swooping Hawks (**Power Rating +5**). A Swooping Hawk Exarch can take the place of one Swooping Hawk. Each model is armed with a lasblaster.

WEAPON	RANGE	TYPE	S	AP	D	ABILITIES
Hawk's talon	24"	Assault 4	5	0	1	-
Lasblaster	24"	Rapid Fire 2	3	0	1	-
Sunrifle	24"	Assault 4	3	-2	1	If a unit suffers any unsaved wounds from this weapon, your opponent must subtract 1 from their hit rolls until the end of the turn.
Power sword	Melee	Melee	User	-3	1	-

WARGEAR OPTIONS	• The Swooping Hawk Exarch may replace their lasblaster with either a hawk's talon or a sunrifle. • The Swooping Hawk Exarch may take a power sword.

ABILITIES	Ancient Doom, Battle Focus (pg 10)

Herald of Victory: You can add 1 to the Leadership of friendly <CRAFTWORLD> units within 3" of any unit that includes a Swooping Hawk Exarch.

Swooping Hawk Grenade Pack: Swooping Hawks can fire a spread of grenades as they fly over enemy units in their Movement phase. To do so, after the unit has moved, pick one enemy unit that they flew over. Then, roll one D6 for each model in the enemy unit (up to a maximum of one dice for each model in the Swooping Hawks unit). Each time you roll a 6 the enemy unit suffers a mortal wound.

Children of Baharroth: During deployment, you can set up a Swooping Hawks unit in the skies instead of placing it on the battlefield. At the end of any of your Movement phases the unit can descend on their Swooping Hawk wings – set them up anywhere on the battlefield that is more than 9" away from any enemy models.

Skyleap: At the beginning of your Movement phase, if this unit is not within 1" of an enemy model they can leap back into the skies. Remove this unit from the battlefield. They can return to the battlefield as described in the Children of Baharroth ability. This unit may not both skyleap and descend on Swooping Hawk wings in the same turn. If the battle ends while this unit is in the skies, they are considered to be slain.

FACTION KEYWORDS	AELDARI, ASURYANI, ASPECT WARRIOR, <CRAFTWORLD>
KEYWORDS	INFANTRY, JUMP PACK, FLY, SWOOPING HAWKS

Swooping Hawks soar into battle, raining blistering fire upon the foe.

WARP SPIDERS

5 POWER

NAME	M	WS	BS	S	T	W	A	Ld	Sv
Warp Spider	7"	3+	3+	3	3	1	1	8	3+
Warp Spider Exarch	7"	3+	3+	3	3	2	2	8	3+

This unit contains 5 Warp Spiders. It can include up to 5 additional Warp Spiders (**Power Rating +5**). A Warp Spider Exarch can take the place of one Warp Spider. Each model is armed with a death spinner.

WEAPON	RANGE	TYPE	S	AP	D	ABILITIES
Death spinner	12"	Assault 2	6	0	1	Each time you make a wound roll of 6+ for this weapon, that hit is resolved with an AP of -4 instead of 0.
Spinneret rifle	18"	Rapid Fire 1	6	-4	1	-
Powerblades	Melee	Melee	User	-2	1	Each time the bearer fights, it can make 1 additional attack with this weapon.

WARGEAR OPTIONS	• The Warp Spider Exarch may replace their death spinner with either two death spinners or a spinneret rifle. • The Warp Spider Exarch may take powerblades.

ABILITIES	**Ancient Doom, Battle Focus** (pg 10) **Warp Jump Generator:** When this unit moves in the Movement phase, they can do so normally or using their warp jump generators. If they use their warp jump generators they cannot Advance or charge this turn, but their Move characteristic is increased by 4D6" and they can **FLY** until the end of the phase.	**Flickerjump:** When a unit with this ability is targeted by a ranged weapon, you can declare that they will make a flickerjump. If they do, your opponent must subtract 1 from hit rolls for attacks that target this unit until the end of the phase. However, you must immediately roll 2D6 – on a 2, one model from the Warp Spiders unit is slain. **Iron Resolve:** A unit that contains a Warp Spider Exarch can re-roll failed Morale tests.

FACTION KEYWORDS	AELDARI, ASURYANI, ASPECT WARRIOR, <CRAFTWORLD>
KEYWORDS	INFANTRY, JUMP PACK, WARP SPIDERS

SHINING SPEARS

7 POWER

NAME	M	WS	BS	S	T	W	A	Ld	Sv
Shining Spear	16"	3+	3+	3	4	2	2	8	3+
Shining Spear Exarch	16"	3+	3+	3	4	3	3	8	3+

This unit contains 3 Shining Spears. It can include up to 3 additional Shining Spears (**Power Rating +7**) or up to 6 additional Shining Spears (**Power Rating +14**). A Shining Spear Exarch can take the place of one Shining Spear. Each model is armed with a laser lance and each of their jetbikes is armed with a twin shuriken catapult.

WEAPON	RANGE	TYPE	S	AP	D	ABILITIES
Laser lance (shooting)	6"	Assault 1	6	-4	2	-
Star lance (shooting)	6"	Assault 1	8	-4	2	-
Twin shuriken catapult	12"	Assault 4	4	0	1	Each time you make a wound roll of 6+ for this weapon, that hit is resolved with an AP of -3 instead of 0.
Laser lance (melee)	Melee	Melee	User	-4	2	If the bearer charged this turn, attacks with this weapon are made at Strength 6.
Paragon blade	Melee	Melee	User	-4	1	You can re-roll failed hit and wound rolls for this weapon.
Star lance (melee)	Melee	Melee	User	-4	2	If the bearer charged this turn, attacks with this weapon are made at Strength 8.

WARGEAR OPTIONS	• The Shining Spear Exarch may replace their laser lance with a star lance or paragon blade.

ABILITIES	**Ancient Doom, Battle Focus** (pg 10) **Ride the Wind:** When this unit Advances, add 6" to its Move characteristic for that Movement phase instead of rolling a dice.	**Aerobatic Grace:** Models in this unit have a 4+ invulnerable save against ranged weapons. **Expert Hunter:** You can re-roll wound rolls for a Shining Spear Exarch when they target a **MONSTER** or **VEHICLE**.

FACTION KEYWORDS	AELDARI, ASURYANI, ASPECT WARRIOR, <CRAFTWORLD>
KEYWORDS	BIKER, FLY, SHINING SPEARS

CRIMSON HUNTER

9 POWER

NAME	M	WS	BS	S	T	W	A	Ld	Sv
Crimson Hunter	*	6+	*	6	6	12	3	8	3+

DAMAGE
Some of this model's characteristics change as it suffers damage, as shown below:

REMAINING W	M	BS
7-12+	20-60"	2+
4-6	20-40"	3+
1-3	20-25"	4+

A Crimson Hunter is a single model equipped with two bright lances and a pulse laser.

WEAPON	RANGE	TYPE	S	AP	D	ABILITIES
Bright lance	36"	Heavy 1	8	-4	D6	-
Pulse laser	48"	Heavy 2	8	-3	3	

ABILITIES

Wings of Khaine: When this model Advances, add 20" to its Move characteristic for that Movement phase instead of rolling a dice. Each time this model moves, first pivot it on the spot up to 90° (this does not contribute to how far the model moves), and then move the model straight forwards. Once its move has finished, you can pivot it a further 90° as before.

Airborne: This model cannot charge, can only be charged by units that can FLY, and can only attack or be attacked in the Fight phase by units that can FLY.

Hard to Hit: Your opponent must subtract 1 from hit rolls for attacks that target this model in the Shooting phase.

Skyhunters: You can re-roll all failed wound rolls for this model's ranged weapons that target units that can FLY.

Crash and Burn: If this model is reduced to 0 wounds, roll a D6 before removing it from the battlefield. On a 6 it crashes in a fiery explosion and each unit within 6" suffers D3 mortal wounds.

FACTION KEYWORDS	AELDARI, ASURYANI, ASPECT WARRIOR, <CRAFTWORLD>
KEYWORDS	VEHICLE, FLY, CRIMSON HUNTER

CRIMSON HUNTER EXARCH

11 POWER

NAME	M	WS	BS	S	T	W	A	Ld	Sv
Crimson Hunter Exarch	*	6+	*	6	6	12	3	8	3+

DAMAGE
Some of this model's characteristics change as it suffers damage, as shown below:

REMAINING W	M	BS
7-12+	20-60"	2+
4-6	20-40"	3+
1-3	20-25"	4+

A Crimson Hunter Exarch is a single model equipped with two bright lances and a pulse laser.

WEAPON	RANGE	TYPE	S	AP	D	ABILITIES
Bright lance	36"	Heavy 1	8	-4	D6	-
Pulse laser	48"	Heavy 2	8	-3	3	-
Starcannon	36"	Heavy 2	6	-3	3	-

WARGEAR OPTIONS	• This model may replace its two bright lances with two starcannons.

ABILITIES

Wings of Khaine: When this model Advances, add 20" to its Move characteristic for that Movement phase instead of rolling a dice. Each time this model moves, first pivot it on the spot up to 90° (this does not contribute to how far the model moves), and then move the model straight forwards. Once its move has finished, you can pivot it a further 90° as before.

Airborne: This model cannot charge, can only be charged by units that can FLY, and can only attack or be attacked in the Fight phase by units that can FLY.

Hard to Hit: Your opponent must subtract 1 from hit rolls for attacks that target this model in the Shooting phase.

Skyhunters: You can re-roll all failed wound rolls for this model's ranged weapons that target units that can FLY.

Marksman's Eye: You can re-roll hit rolls of 1 for this model's ranged weapons.

Crash and Burn: If this model is reduced to 0 wounds, roll a D6 before removing it from the battlefield. On a 6 it crashes in a fiery explosion and each unit within 6" suffers D3 mortal wounds.

FACTION KEYWORDS	AELDARI, ASURYANI, ASPECT WARRIOR, <CRAFTWORLD>
KEYWORDS	VEHICLE, FLY, CRIMSON HUNTER

VYPERS

NAME	M	WS	BS	S	T	W	A	Ld	Sv
Vyper	16"	6+	3+	4	5	6	1	8	3+

This unit contains 1 Vyper. It can include up to 2 additional Vypers (**Power Rating +4 per model**). Each model is armed with a shuriken cannon and a twin shuriken catapult.

WEAPON	RANGE	TYPE	S	AP	D	ABILITIES
Shuriken cannon	24"	Assault 3	6	0	1	Each time you make a wound roll of 6+ for this weapon, that hit is resolved with an AP of -3 instead of 0.
Twin shuriken catapult	12"	Assault 4	4	0	1	Each time you make a wound roll of 6+ for this weapon, that hit is resolved with an AP of -3 instead of 0.

WARGEAR OPTIONS	• Any model may replace its shuriken cannon with a weapon from the *Heavy Weapons* list. • Any model may replace its twin shuriken catapult with a shuriken cannon.

ABILITIES	**Blade Wind:** This unit has a Move characteristic of 20" instead of 16" whilst it contains 3 models.	**Explodes:** If this model is reduced to 0 wounds, roll a D6 before removing it from the battlefield. On a 6 it explodes, and each unit within 3" suffers a mortal wound.

FACTION KEYWORDS	AELDARI, ASURYANI, WARHOST, <CRAFTWORLD>
KEYWORDS	VEHICLE, FLY, VYPERS

HEMLOCK WRAITHFIGHTER

NAME	M	WS	BS	S	T	W	A	Ld	Sv
Hemlock Wraithfighter	∗	6+	∗	6	6	12	3	8	3+

DAMAGE

Some of this model's characteristics change as it suffers damage, as shown below:

REMAINING W	M	BS
7-12+	20-60"	3+
4-6	20-40"	4+
1-3	20-25"	5+

A Hemlock Wraithfighter is a single model equipped with two heavy D-scythes.

WEAPON	RANGE	TYPE	S	AP	D	ABILITIES
Heavy D-scythe	16"	Assault D3	10	-4	2	This weapon automatically hits its target.

ABILITIES	**Wings of Khaine:** When this model Advances, add 20" to its Move characteristic for that Movement phase instead of rolling a dice. Each time this model moves, first pivot it on the spot up to 90° (this does not contribute to how far the model moves), and then move the model straight forwards. Once its move has finished, you can pivot it a further 90° as before. **Airborne:** This model cannot charge, can only be charged by units that can **FLY**, and can only attack or be attacked in the Fight phase by units that can **FLY**. **Hard to Hit:** Your opponent must subtract 1 from hit rolls for attacks that target this model in the Shooting phase.	**Mindshock Pod:** Enemy units within 12" of any Hemlock Wraithfighters subtract 1 from their Leadership characteristic. **Spirit Stones:** Roll a D6 each time this model suffers an unsaved wound or mortal wound: on a 6 the wound is ignored. **Crash and Burn:** If this model is reduced to 0 wounds, roll a D6 before removing it from the battlefield. On a 6 it crashes in a fiery explosion and each unit within 6" suffers D3 mortal wounds.

PSYKER	This model can attempt to manifest one psychic power in each friendly Psychic phase, and attempt to deny one psychic power in each enemy Psychic phase. It knows the *Smite* power and one psychic power from the Runes of Battle discipline (pg 10).

FACTION KEYWORDS	AELDARI, ASURYANI, SPIRIT HOST, <CRAFTWORLD>
KEYWORDS	VEHICLE, FLY, PSYKER, HEMLOCK WRAITHFIGHTER

DARK REAPERS

NAME	M	WS	BS	S	T	W	A	Ld	Sv
Dark Reaper	6"	3+	3+	3	3	1	1	8	3+
Dark Reaper Exarch	6"	3+	3+	3	3	2	2	8	3+

This unit contains 3 Dark Reapers. It can include up to 2 additional Dark Reapers (**Power Rating +4**) or up to 7 additional Dark Reapers (**Power Rating +13**). A Dark Reaper Exarch can take the place of one Dark Reaper. Each model is armed with a reaper launcher.

WEAPON	RANGE	TYPE	S	AP	D	ABILITIES
Aeldari missile launcher	When attacking with this weapon, choose one of the profiles below.					
- Sunburst missile	48"	Heavy D6	4	-1	1	-
- Starshot missile	48"	Heavy 1	8	-2	D6	-
Reaper launcher	When attacking with this weapon, choose one of the profiles below.					
- Starshot missile	48"	Heavy 1	8	-2	3	-
- Starswarm missile	48"	Heavy 2	5	-2	2	-
Shuriken cannon	24"	Assault 3	6	0	1	Each time you make a wound roll of 6+ for this weapon, that hit is resolved with an AP of -3 instead of 0.
Tempest launcher	36"	Heavy 2D6	4	-2	1	This weapon can target units that are not visible to the bearer.

WARGEAR OPTIONS	• The Dark Reaper Exarch may replace their reaper launcher with a shuriken cannon, Aeldari missile launcher or tempest launcher.

ABILITIES	**Ancient Doom** (pg 10) **Crack Shot:** You can re-roll hit rolls of 1 for a Dark Reaper Exarch's ranged weapon.	**Inescapable Accuracy:** Models in this unit always hit on a 3+ when firing a ranged weapon, regardless of any modifiers (although they still only hit on rolls of 6 when firing Overwatch).
FACTION KEYWORDS	**AELDARI, ASURYANI, ASPECT WARRIOR, <CRAFTWORLD>**	
KEYWORDS	**INFANTRY, DARK REAPERS**	

Dark Reapers are sinister destroyers who obliterate their enemies from afar.

VAUL'S WRATH
SUPPORT BATTERY

NAME	M	WS	BS	S	T	W	A	Ld	Sv
Support Weapon	6"	3+	3+	3	5	4	2	7	4+

This unit contains 1 Support Weapon and 2 crew, one manning the weapon and one standing alongside it. It can include up to 2 additional Support Weapons and their crews (**Power Rating +5 per Support Weapon**). Each Support Weapon is equipped with a shadow weaver. In addition, one of its crew can attack with a shuriken catapult.

WEAPON	RANGE	TYPE	S	AP	D	ABILITIES
D-cannon	24"	Heavy D3	10	-4	D6	-
Shadow weaver	48"	Heavy D6	6	0	1	Each time you make a wound roll of 6+ for this weapon, that hit is resolved with an AP of -4 instead of 0. This weapon can target units that are not visible to the bearer.
Shuriken catapult	12"	Assault 2	4	0	1	Each time you make a wound roll of 6+ for this weapon, that hit is resolved with an AP of -3 instead of 0.
Vibro cannon	48"	Heavy 1	7	-1	D3	For each vibro cannon that has already been fired at the same target in this phase, improve the AP of this weapon by 1 (to a maximum of -3) and add 1 to the wound rolls for this weapon (to a maximum of +2). For example, if a firing model is the third to target the same unit with a vibro cannon, its AP is -3 and you add 2 to its wound rolls.

WARGEAR OPTIONS	• Any Support Weapon may replace its shadow weaver with a vibro cannon or a D-cannon.

ABILITIES	**Ancient Doom, Battle Focus** (pg 10) **Support Battery:** A Vaul's Wrath Support Battery must be deployed as a single group with each Support Weapon within 3" of at least one other Support Weapon from their unit, and with each crew within 1" of their Support Weapon. From that point on each Support Weapon acts as a single unit.	**Guardian Crew:** Each Support Weapon and its crew are treated as a single model for all rules purposes. The crew must remain within 1" of their Support Weapon and cannot be targeted or attacked separately. The range and visibility of all attacks made by a Support Weapon and its crew are measured from the Support Weapon, not the crew.

FACTION KEYWORDS	**AELDARI, ASURYANI, WARHOST, <CRAFTWORLD>**
KEYWORDS	**VEHICLE, ARTILLERY, SUPPORT WEAPON**

The massed firepower of the Vaul's Wrath Support Battery is death to any target.

FALCON

11 POWER

NAME	M	WS	BS	S	T	W	A	Ld	Sv
Falcon	✷	6+	✷	6	7	12	✷	8	3+

DAMAGE

Some of this model's characteristics change as it suffers damage, as shown below:

REMAINING W	M	BS	A
7-12+	16"	3+	3
4-6	12"	4+	D3
1-3	8"	5+	1

A Falcon is a single model equipped with a pulse laser, shuriken cannon and a twin shuriken catapult.

WEAPON	RANGE	TYPE	S	AP	D	ABILITIES
Pulse laser	48"	Heavy 2	8	-3	3	-
Shuriken cannon	24"	Assault 3	6	0	1	Each time you make a wound roll of 6+ for this weapon, that hit is resolved with an AP of -3 instead of 0.
Twin shuriken catapult	12"	Assault 4	4	0	1	Each time you make a wound roll of 6+ for this weapon, that hit is resolved with an AP of -3 instead of 0.

WARGEAR OPTIONS	• This model may replace its shuriken cannon with a weapon from the *Heavy Weapons* list. • This model may replace its twin shuriken catapult with a shuriken cannon. • This model may take items from the *Vehicle Equipment* list.
ABILITIES	**Hover Tank:** Distance and ranges are always measured to and from this model's hull, even though it has a base. **Explodes:** If this model is reduced to 0 wounds, roll a D6 before removing it from the battlefield and before any embarked models disembark. On a 6 it explodes, and each unit within 6" suffers D3 mortal wounds.
TRANSPORT	A Falcon can Transport 6 **PHOENIX LORD** or **<CRAFTWORLD>** **INFANTRY** models, other than **JUMP PACK** models. Wraithguard and Wraithblades count as 2 models each.
FACTION KEYWORDS	**AELDARI, ASURYANI, WARHOST, <CRAFTWORLD>**
KEYWORDS	**VEHICLE, TRANSPORT, FLY, FALCON**

FIRE PRISM

9 POWER

NAME	M	WS	BS	S	T	W	A	Ld	Sv
Fire Prism	✷	6+	✷	6	7	12	✷	8	3+

DAMAGE

Some of this model's characteristics change as it suffers damage, as shown below:

REMAINING W	M	BS	A
7-12+	16"	3+	3
4-6	12"	4+	D3
1-3	8"	5+	1

A Fire Prism is a single model equipped with a prism cannon and a twin shuriken catapult.

WEAPON	RANGE	TYPE	S	AP	D	ABILITIES
Prism cannon	When attacking with this weapon, choose one of the profiles below.					
- Dispersed	60"	Heavy D6	6	-3	1	-
- Focused	60"	Heavy D3	9	-4	D3	-
- Lance	60"	Heavy 1	12	-5	D6	-
Shuriken cannon	24"	Assault 3	6	0	1	Each time you make a wound roll of 6+ for this weapon, that hit is resolved with an AP of -3 instead of 0.
Twin shuriken catapult	12"	Assault 4	4	0	1	Each time you make a wound roll of 6+ for this weapon, that hit is resolved with an AP of -3 instead of 0.

WARGEAR OPTIONS	• This model may replace its twin shuriken catapult with a shuriken cannon. • This model may take items from the *Vehicle Equipment* list.
ABILITIES	**Hover Tank:** Distance and ranges are always measured to and from this model's hull, even though it has a base. **Explodes:** If this model is reduced to 0 wounds, roll a D6 before removing it from the battlefield. On a 6 it explodes, and each unit within 6" suffers D3 mortal wounds.
FACTION KEYWORDS	**AELDARI, ASURYANI, WARHOST, <CRAFTWORLD>**
KEYWORDS	**VEHICLE, FLY, FIRE PRISM**

NIGHT SPINNER

9 POWER

NAME	M	WS	BS	S	T	W	A	Ld	Sv
Night Spinner	*	6+	*	6	7	12	*	8	3+

DAMAGE
Some of this model's characteristics change as it suffers damage, as shown below:

REMAINING W	M	BS	A
7-12+	16"	3+	3
4-6	12"	4+	D3
1-3	8"	5+	1

A Night Spinner is a single model equipped with a doomweaver and a twin shuriken catapult.

WEAPON	RANGE	TYPE	S	AP	D	ABILITIES
Doomweaver	48"	Heavy 2D6	7	0	2	Wound rolls of 6+ for this weapon are resolved with AP -4 instead of AP 0. This weapon can target units that are not visible to the bearer.
Shuriken cannon	24"	Assault 3	6	0	1	Each time you make a wound roll of 6+ for this weapon, that hit is resolved with an AP of -3 instead of 0.
Twin shuriken catapult	12"	Assault 4	4	0	1	Each time you make a wound roll of 6+ for this weapon, that hit is resolved with an AP of -3 instead of 0.

WARGEAR OPTIONS	• This model may replace its twin shuriken catapult with a shuriken cannon. • This model may take items from the *Vehicle Equipment* list.

ABILITIES	**Hover Tank:** Distance and ranges are always measured to and from this model's hull, even though it has a base.	**Explodes:** If this model is reduced to 0 wounds, roll a D6 before removing it from the battlefield. On a 6 it explodes, and each unit within 6" suffers D3 mortal wounds.

FACTION KEYWORDS	AELDARI, ASURYANI, WARHOST, <CRAFTWORLD>
KEYWORDS	VEHICLE, FLY, NIGHT SPINNER

WAR WALKERS

5 POWER

NAME	M	WS	BS	S	T	W	A	Ld	Sv
War Walker	10"	3+	3+	5	6	6	2	8	4+

This unit contains 1 War Walker. It can include 1 additional War Walker (**Power Rating +5**) or 2 additional War Walkers (**Power Rating +10**). Each model is armed with two shuriken cannons.

WEAPON	RANGE	TYPE	S	AP	D	ABILITIES
Shuriken cannon	24"	Assault 3	6	0	1	Each time you make a wound roll of 6+ for this weapon, that hit is resolved with an AP of -3 instead of 0.

WARGEAR OPTIONS	• Any model may replace its shuriken cannons with two items from the *Heavy Weapons* list.

ABILITIES	**Ancient Doom, Battle Focus** (pg 10) **Scout Vehicle:** At the start of the first battle round, but before the first turn begins, you can move this model up to 12" in any direction, provided that it does not end this move within 9" of any enemy models.	**Power Field:** Models in this unit have a 5+ invulnerable save. **Explodes:** If this model is reduced to 0 wounds, roll a D6 before removing it from the battlefield. On a 6 it explodes, and each unit within 3" suffers a mortal wound.

FACTION KEYWORDS	AELDARI, ASURYANI, WARHOST, <CRAFTWORLD>
KEYWORDS	VEHICLE, WAR WALKERS

WRAITHLORD

7 POWER

NAME	M	WS	BS	S	T	W	A	Ld	Sv
Wraithlord	*	*	*	7	7	10	3	9	3+

A Wraithlord is a single model armed with two shuriken catapults and wraithbone fists.

WEAPON	RANGE	TYPE	S	AP	D	ABILITIES
Flamer	8"	Assault D6	4	0	1	This weapon automatically hits its target.
Shuriken catapult	12"	Assault 2	4	0	1	Each time you make a wound roll of 6+ for this weapon, that hit is resolved with an AP of -3 instead of 0.
Ghostglaive	Melee	Melee	+2	-4	D6	-
Wraithbone fists	Melee	Melee	User	-3	3	-

DAMAGE
Some of this model's characteristics change as it suffers damage, as shown below:

REMAINING W	M	WS	BS
6-10+	8"	3+	3+
3-5	7"	4+	4+
1-2	6"	5+	5+

WARGEAR OPTIONS	• This model may replace any shuriken catapult with a flamer. • This model may take a ghostglaive. • This model may take up to two items from the *Heavy Weapons* list.
ABILITIES	Ancient Doom (pg 10)
FACTION KEYWORDS	AELDARI, ASURYANI, SPIRIT HOST, <CRAFTWORLD>
KEYWORDS	MONSTER, WRAITHLORD

WRAITHKNIGHT

27 POWER

NAME	M	WS	BS	S	T	W	A	Ld	Sv
Wraithknight	*	*	*	8	8	24	4	9	3+

A Wraithknight is a single model armed with two heavy wraithcannons, titanic wraithbone fists and titanic feet.

WEAPON	RANGE	TYPE	S	AP	D	ABILITIES
Heavy wraithcannon	36"	Assault 2	10	-4	D6	-
Scatter laser	36"	Heavy 4	6	0	1	-
Shuriken cannon	24"	Assault 3	6	0	1	Each time you make a wound roll of 6+ for this weapon, that hit is resolved with an AP of -3 instead of 0.
Starcannon	36"	Heavy 2	6	-3	3	-
Suncannon	48"	Heavy 2D6	6	-3	D3	-
Titanic feet	Melee	Melee	User	-2	D3	When you make an attack with this weapon, roll 3 dice instead of 1.
Titanic ghostglaive	Melee	Melee	x2	-4	6	-
Titanic wraithbone fists	Melee	Melee	User	-3	D6	-

DAMAGE
Some of this model's characteristics change as it suffers damage, as shown below:

REMAINING W	M	WS	BS
13-24+	12"	3+	3+
7-12	10"	4+	4+
1-6	8"	5+	5+

WARGEAR OPTIONS	• This model may replace its heavy wraithcannons with either a titanic ghostglaive and scattershield or a suncannon and scattershield.
	• This model may take up to two items from the following:
	  - Scatter laser
	  - Shuriken cannon
	  - Starcannon

ABILITIES	Ancient Doom (pg 10) **Scattershield:** A model equipped with a scattershield has a 5+ invulnerable save. **Catastrophic Collapse:** If this model is reduced to 0 wounds, roll a D6 before removing it from the battlefield. On a 6 it collapses with catastrophic effect, and each unit within 2D6" suffers D6 mortal wounds. **Unstoppable Revenant:** A Wraithknight can Fall Back in the Movement phase and still shoot and/or charge during its turn. When a Wraithknight Falls Back, it can even move over enemy INFANTRY models, though at the end of its move it must be more than 1" from all enemy units. In addition, a Wraithknight can move and fire Heavy weapons without suffering the penalty to its hit rolls. Finally, a Wraithknight only gains a bonus to its save in cover if at least half of the model is obscured from the firer.
FACTION KEYWORDS	AELDARI, ASURYANI, SPIRIT HOST, <CRAFTWORLD>
KEYWORDS	MONSTER, TITANIC, WRAITHKNIGHT

Elegant and deadly, the Wraithknight towers over the enemy as it unleashes annihilation upon them.

DRUKHARI

The Drukhari are a race of sadistic killers who feed upon the exquisite agony of their victims. From the Dark City of Commorragh, hidden deep within the twisting passages of the webway, their reaver-fleets strike forth in a never-ending search for new souls to torment.

Selfish and capricious creatures, the Drukhari fight only to satisfy their insatiable thirst for the agonies of lesser beings. Though they are as physically graceful, even beautiful, as their craftworld cousins, one only has to witness the horror of a Drukhari raiding party to understand the foulness that infests their black hearts. Fleet-footed warriors clad in barbed armour spill from dagger-like skiffs, their cruel weapons spitting a hail of toxin-laced crystals that leave their victims convulsing in unimaginable agony. Lashes and flensing blades tear into flesh as whooping figures dance and leap into battle, always looking for the agonising strike ahead of the killing blow. As the enemy is driven to ever greater heights of terror, still darker creatures emerge from the gloom – deformed, stitch-fleshed abominations with wicked scythe-limbs, whose pallid forms ripple with unnatural muscle. These twisted beasts are led forth by skeletal figures who drift eerily across the battlefield, eyes glimmering with malicious delight.

The origins of the Drukhari stretch back to the height of the ancient Aeldari empire, many centuries before the Fall. With their domination of the galaxy uncontested and their mastery of science rendering self-improvement and cultural evolution redundant, the Aeldari turned their minds to personal gratification and the pursuit of individual pleasure. Cults of excess began to rise in influence all across the empire, dominated by the ancient noble bloodlines who could afford to indulge in every aspect of decadence. The port city of Commorragh, nestled deep within the webway, became

the centre of this dark practise. When the accumulated vice of the Aeldari ultimately led to their downfall and the birth of She Who Thirsts, the occluded pathways of the webway prevented those who dwelt in the Dark City from the terrible fate that befell their kin.

Yet the Commorrites did not escape entirely unscathed. Rather than having their souls torn apart and devoured in an instant, they were instead subjected to the slow draining of their essence as Slaanesh siphoned it away. It was only by parasitically stealing animus from helpless victims that the Aeldari of Commorragh could escape their damnation. The pain of others nourished their broken, withered souls, and as long as they could maintain a regular supply of enemies and slaves to practice their tortures upon, they could live on for millennia, safe from the hunger of the god they helped bring into being. Thus, the Drukhari were born, a race of sadistic parasites whose cruelty has damned them to an eternity of ghoulish hunger.

The Drukhari dwell within the inter-dimensional metropolis of Commorragh still, and their raiding fleets sail forth constantly in search of fresh slaves. Like their craftworld cousins, the Drukhari make use of the labyrinthine pathways of the webway to emerge undetected, and therefore it is almost impossible to predict where they might strike next. Those who have heard tales of the Drukhari's sadistic tortures know that it is far better to fall in battle against them than it is to be taken alive.

THE DARK CITY

Commorragh is a vast metropolis, the true size of which is utterly incomprehensible. It stretches across many transdimensional paths and satellite realms and houses a population whose numbers are impossible to gauge. One corner of the Dark City may in fact be several thousand light years away from another, yet shimmering dimensional pathways provide swift travel to its citizens.

Those who approach Commorragh are met by a sprawling forest of foreboding spires and starscrapers, threaded by the flaring engine-trails of thousands of vessels. The baleful glow of dead suns washes the city's streets and underwarrens in a sickly yellow-grey light, and the impossibly tall structures that dominate the skyline are bedecked with darkly majestic statuary.

The rings of the inner city and the tallest spires of Commorragh are home to the warring Kabals, whose games of political intrigue and backstabbing are as vicious and bloody as any war. The lower city and its outskirts are lawless, dominated by jetbike gangs and hired killers, constantly echoing with the sounds of battle and the screams of tormented slaves.

The Dark City is surrounded by shimmering portals that lead into the depths of the webway, and the Drukhari's insatiable appetites ensure that an almost constant stream of raiding parties pours forth into these gateways, spreading the cruelty and terror of Commorragh across the galaxy.

DRUKHARI ARMY LIST

This section contains all of the datasheets that you will need in order to fight battles with your Drukhari miniatures. Each datasheet includes the characteristics profiles of the unit it describes, as well as any wargear and abilities it may have. Some rules are common to several Drukhari units – these are described below and referenced on the datasheets.

ABILITIES

The following abilities are common to several Drukhari units:

Power From Pain

All **DRUKHARI** units with this ability gain a bonus depending upon which battle round it is, as shown in the table below.

POWER FROM PAIN	
BATTLE ROUND	**BONUS***
1	**Inured to Suffering:** Roll a D6 each time a model with this ability suffers a wound. On a 6, it ignores the injury and the wound is not lost.
2	**Eager to Flay:** You can re-roll the dice when determining how far a unit with this ability moves when it Advances or charges.
3	**Flensing Fury:** You can add 1 to hit rolls made for a unit with this ability in the Fight phase.
4	**Emboldened by Bloodshed:** Units with this ability automatically pass Morale tests (do not roll the dice).
5+	**Mantle of Agony:** Subtract 1 from the Leadership of enemy units that are within 6" of any units with this ability in the Morale phase.

* All bonuses are cumulative. For example, in the second battle round, wounds are ignored on a roll of 6, and you can re-roll the distance when a unit Advances or charges.

Combat Drugs

Units with this ability gain a bonus during the battle depending on the drugs injected into their veins. Before the battle, roll on the combat drug table to see which combat drug the unit is using. Alternatively, you can pick the bonus the unit receives, but if you do this you cannot choose a bonus that has already been taken by another unit until all six combat drugs have been taken once each.

COMBAT DRUGS	
D6	**BONUS**
1	**Adrenalight:** +1 Attack
2	**Grave Lotus:** +1 Strength
3	**Hypex:** +2 Move
4	**Painbringer:** +1 Toughness
5	**Serpentin:** +1 Weapon Skill (i.e. WS 3+ becomes WS 2+)
6	**Splintermind:** +2 Leadership

KEYWORDS

Throughout this section you will come across a keyword that is within angular brackets, for example <**KABAL**>. This is shorthand for a keyword of your own choosing, as described below.

<KABAL>, <WYCH CULT> AND <HAEMONCULUS COVEN>

Most Drukhari belong to either a Kabal, or a Wych Cult or a Haemonculus Coven. Some datasheets specify what Kabal, Wych Cult or Haemonculus Coven the unit is drawn from (e.g. Lelith Hesperax has the **WYCH CULT OF STRIFE** keyword). Other **DRUKHARI** datasheets may have either the <**KABAL**>, <**WYCH CULT**> or <**HAEMONCULUS COVEN**> keyword. When you include such a unit in your army, you must nominate which Kabal, Wych Cult or Haemonculus Coven the unit is from. You then simply replace the <**KABAL**>, <**HAEMONCULUS COVEN**>, or <**WYCH CULT**> keyword in every instance on that unit's datasheet with the name you chose.

For example, if you were to include an Archon in your army, and you decided the Archon was from the Kabal of the Black Heart, then their <**KABAL**> Faction keyword would be changed to **KABAL OF THE BLACK HEART** and their Overlord ability would then say 'All friendly **KABAL OF THE BLACK HEART** units that are within 6" of this model can use its Leadership instead of their own.'

WARGEAR

Many of the units you will find on the following pages reference one or more of the following wargear lists. When this is the case, the unit may take any item from the appropriate list below. The profiles for the weapons in these lists can be found in the appendix (pg 120-122).

TOOLS OF TORMENT

A model may replace a ranged weapon with a single weapon from this list:
- Hexrifle
- Liquifier gun
- Stinger pistol

WEAPONS OF TORTURE

A model may replace a melee weapon with a single weapon from this list:
- Agoniser
- Electrocorrosive whip
- Flesh gauntlet
- Mindphase gauntlet
- Scissorhand
- Venom blade

ARCHON

4 POWER

NAME	M	WS	BS	S	T	W	A	Ld	Sv
Archon	8"	2+	2+	3	3	5	5	9	5+

An Archon is a single model armed with a splinter pistol and a huskblade.

WEAPON	RANGE	TYPE	S	AP	D	ABILITIES
Blast pistol	6"	Pistol 1	8	-4	D3	-
Blaster	18"	Assault 1	8	-4	D3	-
Phantasm grenade launcher	18"	Assault D3	1	0	1	If a unit is hit by one or more phantasm grenade launchers, subtract one from its Leadership until the end of the turn.
Splinter pistol	12"	Pistol 1	*	0	1	This weapon wounds on a 4+, unless it is targeting a **Vehicle**, in which case it wounds on a 6+.
Agoniser	Melee	Melee	*	-2	1	This weapon wounds on a 4+, unless it is targeting a **Vehicle**, in which case it wounds on a 6+.
Huskblade	Melee	Melee	User	-2	D3	-
Power sword	Melee	Melee	User	-3	1	-

WARGEAR OPTIONS	• This model may take a phantasm grenade launcher. • This model may replace its huskblade with an agoniser or power sword. • This model may replace its splinter pistol with a blast pistol or blaster.

ABILITIES	**Power From Pain** (pg 42) **Shadowfield:** This model has a 2+ invulnerable save which cannot be re-rolled for any reason. The first time this invulnerable save is failed the shadowfield ceases to function for the remainder of the battle.	**Overlord:** All friendly <**Kabal**> units that are within 6" of this model can use its Leadership instead of their own.

FACTION KEYWORDS	**Aeldari, Drukhari, <Kabal>**
KEYWORDS	**Character, Infantry, Archon**

LHAMAEAN

2 POWER

NAME	M	WS	BS	S	T	W	A	Ld	Sv
Lhamaean	8"	3+	3+	3	3	3	2	8	5+

A Lhamaean is a single model armed with a splinter pistol and a shaimeshi blade.

WEAPON	RANGE	TYPE	S	AP	D	ABILITIES
Splinter pistol	12"	Pistol 1	*	0	1	This weapon wounds on a 4+, unless it is targeting a **Vehicle**, in which case it wounds on a 6+.
Shaimeshi blade	Melee	Melee	*	0	1	This weapon wounds on a 2+, unless it is targeting a **Vehicle**, in which case it wounds on a 6+. Each time you roll a wound roll of 6+ for this weapon, other than against a **Vehicle**, the target suffers a mortal wound in addition to any other damage.

ABILITIES	**Power From Pain** (pg 42) **Court of the Archon:** You can re-roll failed hit rolls with this model whilst it is within 3" of a friendly <**Kabal**> **Archon**. In addition, if your army is Battle-forged, then for each Archon in your army you can take up to four models with this ability in the same Detachment without taking up any of the Detachment's slots.

FACTION KEYWORDS	**Aeldari, Drukhari, <Kabal>**
KEYWORDS	**Character, Infantry, Lhamaean**

MEDUSAE

2 POWER

NAME	M	WS	BS	S	T	W	A	Ld	Sv
Medusae	8"	3+	3+	3	3	3	1	8	5+

A Medusae is a single model which attacks with an eyeburst.

WEAPON	RANGE	TYPE	S	AP	D	ABILITIES
Eyeburst	9"	Assault 4	4	-2	1	-

ABILITIES	**Power From Pain** (pg 42) **Court of the Archon:** You can re-roll failed hit rolls with this model whilst it is within 3" of a friendly <Kabal> Archon. In addition, if your army is Battle-forged, then for each Archon in your army you can take up to four models with this ability in the same Detachment without taking up any of the Detachment's slots.
FACTION KEYWORDS	Aeldari, Drukhari, <Kabal>
KEYWORDS	Character, Infantry, Medusae

SSLYTH

3 POWER

NAME	M	WS	BS	S	T	W	A	Ld	Sv
Sslyth	8"	3+	3+	5	5	4	3	2	5+

A Sslyth is a single model equipped with a shardcarbine, splinter pistol and Sslyth battle-blade.

WEAPON	RANGE	TYPE	S	AP	D	ABILITIES
Shardcarbine	18"	Assault 3	*	0	1	This weapon wounds on a 4+, unless it is targeting a **Vehicle**, in which case it wounds on a 6+.
Splinter pistol	12"	Pistol 1	*	0	1	This weapon wounds on a 4+, unless it is targeting a **Vehicle**, in which case it wounds on a 6+.
Sslyth battle-blade	Melee	Melee	User	-1	1	-

ABILITIES	**Insensible To Pain:** A Sslyth has a 5+ invulnerable save. **Cold-blooded Bodyguard:** Roll a D6 each time a <Kabal> Archon loses a wound whilst they are within 3" of this model; on a 2+ this model intercepts that hit – the Archon does not lose a wound but this model suffers a mortal wound.	**Court of the Archon:** You can re-roll failed hit rolls with this model whilst it is within 3" of a friendly <Kabal> Archon. In addition, if your army is Battle-forged, then for each Archon in your army you can take up to four models with this ability in the same Detachment without taking up any of the Detachment's slots.
FACTION KEYWORDS	Aeldari, Drukhari, <Kabal>	
KEYWORDS	Character, Infantry, Sslyth	

Archons surround themselves with deadly specialists and lethal 'pets'.

UR-GHUL

2 POWER

NAME	M	WS	BS	S	T	W	A	Ld	Sv
Ur-Ghul	8"	3+	-	4	3	3	4	2	7+

An Ur-Ghul is a single model which attacks with claws and talons.

WEAPON	RANGE	TYPE	S	AP	D	ABILITIES
Claws and talons	Melee	Melee	User	0	1	-

ABILITIES		
Insensible To Pain: An Ur-Ghul has a 5+ invulnerable save. **Ferocious Charge:** Add 2 to an Ur-Ghul's Attacks characteristic if it charged in the same turn.		**Court of the Archon:** You can re-roll failed hit rolls with this model whilst it is within 3" of a friendly <KABAL> ARCHON. In addition, if your army is Battle-forged, then for each Archon in your army you can take up to four models with this ability in the same Detachment without taking up any of the Detachment's slots.

FACTION KEYWORDS	AELDARI, DRUKHARI, <KABAL>
KEYWORDS	CHARACTER, INFANTRY, UR-GHUL

SUCCUBUS

4 POWER

NAME	M	WS	BS	S	T	W	A	Ld	Sv
Succubus	8"	2+	2+	3	3	5	4	8	6+

A Succubus is a single model armed with a splinter pistol and an archite glaive.

WEAPON	RANGE	TYPE	S	AP	D	ABILITIES
Blast pistol	6"	Pistol 1	8	-4	D3	-
Splinter pistol	12"	Pistol 1	*	0	1	This weapon wounds on a 4+, unless it is targeting a VEHICLE, in which case it wounds on a 6+.
Agoniser	Melee	Melee	*	-2	1	This weapon wounds on a 4+, unless it is targeting a VEHICLE, in which case it wounds on a 6+.
Archite glaive	Melee	Melee	+2	-3	1	When attacking with this weapon, you must subtract 1 from the hit roll.
Impaler	Melee	Melee	User	-1	2	-

WARGEAR OPTIONS	• This model may replace its splinter pistol with an agoniser, blast pistol or impaler.

ABILITIES		
Power From Pain, Combat Drugs (pg 42) **Brides of Death:** In the Fight phase you can re-roll all hit rolls of 1 made for friendly <WYCH CULT> units that are within 6" of this model.		**Lightning Dodge:** This model has a 4+ invulnerable save. **No Escape:** Roll off if an enemy INFANTRY unit within 1" of any models with this ability wishes to Fall Back. The enemy unit can only Fall Back if the player commanding it wins the roll-off.

FACTION KEYWORDS	AELDARI, DRUKHARI, <WYCH CULT>
KEYWORDS	CHARACTER, INFANTRY, SUCCUBUS

7 POWER

LELITH HESPERAX

NAME	M	WS	BS	S	T	W	A	Ld	Sv
Lelith Hesperax	8"	2+	2+	3	3	5	4	8	6+

Lelith Hesperax is a single model armed with two penetrating blades and a mane of barbs and hooks. Only one of this model may be included in your army.

WEAPON	RANGE	TYPE	S	AP	D	ABILITIES
Impaler	Melee	Melee	User	-1	2	-
Mane of barbs and hooks	Melee	Melee	User	0	1	Each time the bearer fights, it can make 2 additional attacks with this weapon.
Penetrating blade	Melee	Melee	User	-4	1	A model armed with two penetrating blades can make 1 additional attack with them each time it fights.

WARGEAR OPTIONS	• Lelith Hesperax may replace one penetrating blade with an impaler.

ABILITIES	**Power From Pain, Combat Drugs** (pg 42)	**No Escape:** Roll off if an enemy **INFANTRY** unit within 1" of any models with this ability wishes to Fall Back. The enemy unit can only Fall Back if the player commanding it wins the roll-off.
	A League Apart: Lelith Hesperax re-rolls all failed hit and wound rolls when attacking enemy **CHARACTERS** in the Fight phase.	
	Brides of Death: In the Fight phase you can re-roll all hit rolls of 1 made for friendly **WYCH CULT OF STRIFE** units that are within 6" of Lelith Hesperax.	**Quicksilver Dodge:** Lelith Hesperax has a 3+ invulnerable save.

FACTION KEYWORDS	**AELDARI, DRUKHARI, WYCH CULT OF STRIFE**
KEYWORDS	**CHARACTER, INFANTRY, SUCCUBUS, LELITH HESPERAX**

5 POWER

HAEMONCULUS

NAME	M	WS	BS	S	T	W	A	Ld	Sv
Haemonculus	7"	2+	2+	3	4	5	5	8	6+

A Haemonculus is a single model armed with a splinter pistol and Haemonculus tools.

WEAPON	RANGE	TYPE	S	AP	D	ABILITIES
Splinter pistol	12"	Pistol 1	*	0	1	This weapon wounds on a 4+, unless it is targeting a **VEHICLE**, in which case it wounds on a 6+.
Haemonculus tools	Melee	Melee	*	0	1	This weapon wounds on a 4+, unless it is targeting a **VEHICLE**, in which case it wounds on a 6+.

WARGEAR OPTIONS	• This model may take items from the *Weapons of Torture* and/or *Tools of Torment* lists. • This model may take a crucible of malediction.

ABILITIES	**Power From Pain** (pg 42)	**Crucible of Malediction:** A Haemonculus with a crucible of malediction can unleash its contents once per battle, in its Psychic phase. If it does so, roll a D6 for each **PSYKER** within 12" of this model; on a roll of 4+, the unit being rolled for suffers D3 mortal wounds.
	Insensible To Pain: This model has a 5+ invulnerable save.	
	Master of Pain: Add 1 to the Toughness of friendly **<HAEMONCULUS COVEN>** units within 6" of one or more models with this ability.	

FACTION KEYWORDS	**AELDARI, DRUKHARI, <HAEMONCULUS COVEN>**
KEYWORDS	**CHARACTER, INFANTRY, HAEMONCULUS**

URIEN RAKARTH

6 POWER

NAME	M	WS	BS	S	T	W	A	Ld	Sv
Urien Rakarth	7"	2+	2+	3	5	5	4	8	6+

Urien Rakarth is a single model armed with the Casket of Flensing, Haemonculus tools and an ichor injector. Only one of this model may be included in your army.

WEAPON	RANGE	TYPE	S	AP	D	ABILITIES
Casket of Flensing	12"	Assault 2D6	3	-2	1	This weapon can only be fired once per battle.
Haemonculus tools	Melee	Melee	*	0	1	This weapon wounds on a 4+, unless it is targeting a **VEHICLE**, in which case it wounds on a 6+.
Ichor injector	Melee	Melee	User	0	1	The bearer can make a maximum of one attack with the ichor injector each turn (any remaining attacks must be made with a different melee weapon). You can re-roll wound rolls for this weapon. Each time you roll a wound roll of 6+ for this weapon, the target suffers D3 mortal wounds in addition to any other damage.

ABILITIES	Power From Pain (pg 42) **Clone Field:** Urien Rakarth has a 4+ invulnerable save. **Contempt for Death:** You can re-roll failed save rolls for Urien Rakarth against attacks that have a Strength of less than 9.	**Master of Pain:** Add 1 to the Toughness of friendly **PROPHETS OF FLESH** units within 6" of one or more models with this ability.
FACTION KEYWORDS	**AELDARI, DRUKHARI, PROPHETS OF FLESH**	
KEYWORDS	**CHARACTER, INFANTRY, HAEMONCULUS, URIEN RAKARTH**	

DRAZHAR

7 POWER

NAME	M	WS	BS	S	T	W	A	Ld	Sv
Drazhar	7"	2+	2+	4	4	5	4	9	2+

Drazhar is a single model armed with demiklaives. Only one of this model may be included in your army.

WEAPON	RANGE	TYPE	S	AP	D	ABILITIES
Demiklaives	Each time this model fights, choose one of the profiles below.					
- Single blade	Melee	Melee	+1	-3	1	-
- Dual blades	Melee	Melee	User	-2	1	A model attacking with dual blades can make 2 additional attacks with them each time it fights.

ABILITIES	Power From Pain (pg 42) **Eternal Warrior:** Drazhar has a 5+ invulnerable save. **Master of Blades:** Add 1 to the hit rolls of all friendly **INCUBI** units that are within 6" of Drazhar when they fight in the Fight phase.	**Murderous Assault:** Each time Drazhar rolls a wound roll of 6+ in the Fight phase, he may make 1 additional attack. These extra attacks cannot generate any additional attacks.
FACTION KEYWORDS	**AELDARI, DRUKHARI, INCUBI**	
KEYWORDS	**CHARACTER, INFANTRY, DRAZHAR**	

KABALITE WARRIORS

NAME	M	WS	BS	S	T	W	A	Ld	Sv
Kabalite Warrior	7"	3+	3+	3	3	1	1	7	5+
Sybarite	7"	3+	3+	3	3	1	2	8	5+

This unit contains 1 Sybarite and 4 Kabalite Warriors. It can include up to 5 additional Kabalite Warriors (**Power Rating +2**), up to 10 additional Kabalite Warriors (**Power Rating +4**) or up to 15 additional Kabalite Warriors (**Power Rating +6**). Each model is equipped with a splinter rifle.

WEAPON	RANGE	TYPE	S	AP	D	ABILITIES
Blast pistol	6"	Pistol 1	8	-4	D3	-
Blaster	18"	Assault 1	8	-4	D3	-
Dark lance	36"	Heavy 1	8	-4	D6	-
Phantasm grenade launcher	18"	Assault D3	1	0	1	If a unit is hit by one or more phantasm grenade launchers, subtract one from its Leadership until the end of the turn.
Shredder	12"	Assault D3	6	0	1	When attacking a unit of **INFANTRY**, you can re-roll failed wound rolls for this weapon.
Splinter cannon	36"	Rapid Fire 3	*	0	1	Splinter weapons wound on a 4+, unless they are targeting a **VEHICLE**, in which case they wound on a 6+.
Splinter pistol	12"	Pistol 1	*	0	1	
Splinter rifle	24"	Rapid Fire 1	*	0	1	
Agoniser	Melee	Melee	*	-2	1	This weapon wounds on a 4+, unless it is targeting a **VEHICLE**, in which case it wounds on a 6+.
Power sword	Melee	Melee	User	-3	1	-

WARGEAR OPTIONS	• The Sybarite may take a power sword or agoniser. • The Sybarite may take a phantasm grenade launcher. • The Sybarite may replace their splinter rifle with a splinter pistol or a blast pistol. • For every 10 models in the unit, one Kabalite Warrior may replace their splinter rifle with a splinter cannon or dark lance. • One model may replace its splinter rifle with a shredder or a blaster. If the unit includes 20 models, one other model may also do this.
ABILITIES	**Power From Pain** (pg 42)
FACTION KEYWORDS	**AELDARI, DRUKHARI, <KABAL>**
KEYWORDS	**INFANTRY, KABALITE WARRIORS**

The array of fearsome weapons borne by the Kabalite Warriors renders them deadly indeed.

KABALITE TRUEBORN

NAME	M	WS	BS	S	T	W	A	Ld	Sv
Kabalite Trueborn	7"	3+	3+	3	3	1	2	8	5+
Dracon	7"	3+	3+	3	3	1	3	8	5+

This unit contains 1 Dracon and 4 Kabalite Trueborn. It can include up to 5 additional Kabalite Trueborn (**Power Rating +3**), up to 10 additional Kabalite Trueborn (**Power Rating +6**) or up to 15 additional Kabalite Trueborn (**Power Rating +9**). Each model is equipped with a splinter rifle.

WEAPON	RANGE	TYPE	S	AP	D	ABILITIES
Blast pistol	6"	Pistol 1	8	-4	D3	-
Blaster	18"	Assault 1	8	-4	D3	-
Dark lance	36"	Heavy 1	8	-4	D6	-
Phantasm grenade launcher	18"	Assault D3	1	0	1	If a unit is hit by one or more phantasm grenade launchers, subtract one from its Leadership until the end of the turn.
Shredder	12"	Assault D3	6	0	1	When attacking a unit of **INFANTRY**, you can re-roll failed wound rolls for this weapon.
Splinter cannon	36"	Rapid Fire 3	*	0	1	Splinter weapons wound on a 4+, unless they are targeting a **VEHICLE**, in which case they wound on a 6+.
Splinter pistol	12"	Pistol 1	*	0	1	
Splinter rifle	24"	Rapid Fire 1	*	0	1	
Agoniser	Melee	Melee	*	-2	1	This weapon wounds on a 4+, unless it is targeting a **VEHICLE**, in which case it wounds on a 6+.
Power sword	Melee	Melee	User	-3	1	-

WARGEAR OPTIONS	• The Dracon may take a power sword or agoniser. • The Dracon may take a phantasm grenade launcher. • The Dracon may replace their splinter rifle with a splinter pistol or blast pistol. • Up to two Kabalite Trueborn may replace their splinter rifles with a splinter cannon or dark lance. • Up to four Kabalite Trueborn may replace their splinter rifles with a shredder or blaster.
ABILITIES	Power From Pain (pg 42)
FACTION KEYWORDS	AELDARI, DRUKHARI, <KABAL>
KEYWORDS	INFANTRY, KABALITE TRUEBORN

WYCHES

NAME	M	WS	BS	S	T	W	A	Ld	Sv
Wych	8"	3+	3+	3	3	1	1	7	6+
Hekatrix	8"	3+	3+	3	3	1	2	8	6+

This unit contains 1 Hekatrix and 4 Wyches. It can include up to 5 additional Wyches (**Power Rating +3**), up to 10 additional Wyches (**Power Rating +5**) or up to 15 additional Wyches (**Power Rating +7**). Each model is equipped with a splinter pistol, Hekatarii blade and darklight grenades.

WEAPON	RANGE	TYPE	S	AP	D	ABILITIES
Blast pistol	6"	Pistol 1	8	-4	D3	-
Phantasm grenade launcher	18"	Assault D3	1	0	1	If a unit is hit by one or more phantasm grenade launchers, subtract one from its Leadership until the end of the turn.
Splinter pistol	12"	Pistol 1	*	0	1	This weapon wounds on a 4+, unless it is targeting a **VEHICLE**, in which case it wounds on a 6+.
Agoniser	Melee	Melee	*	-2	1	This weapon wounds on a 4+, unless it is targeting a **VEHICLE**, in which case it wounds on a 6+.
Hekatarii blade	Melee	Melee	User	0	1	Each time the bearer fights, it can make 1 additional attack with this weapon.
Hydra gauntlets	Melee	Melee	User	-1	1	Each time the bearer fights, it can make 1 additional attack with this weapon. You can re-roll failed wound rolls for this weapon.
Power sword	Melee	Melee	User	-3	1	-
Razorflails	Melee	Melee	User	-1	1	Each time the bearer fights, it can make 1 additional attack with this weapon. You can re-roll failed hit rolls for this weapon.
Shardnet and impaler	Melee	Melee	User	-1	2	-
Darklight grenade	6"	Grenade D6	4	-1	1	-

WARGEAR OPTIONS	• The Hekatrix may take a phantasm grenade launcher. • The Hekatrix may replace their splinter pistol with a blast pistol. • The Hekatrix may replace their Hekatarii blade with a power sword or an agoniser. • One Wych may replace their splinter pistol and Hekatarii blade with either razorflails, hydra gauntlets, or a shardnet and impaler. If the unit numbers 10 or more models, up to two further Wyches can also do this.

ABILITIES	**Power From Pain, Combat Drugs** (pg 42) **Dodge:** Models in this unit have a 4+ invulnerable save in the Fight phase.	**No Escape:** Roll off if an enemy **INFANTRY** unit within 1" of any models with this ability wishes to Fall Back. The enemy unit can only Fall Back if the player commanding it wins the roll-off.
FACTION KEYWORDS	**AELDARI, DRUKHARI, <WYCH CULT>**	
KEYWORDS	**INFANTRY, WYCHES**	

Drukhari Wyches sprint into battle, shrieking with hateful glee.

HEKATRIX BLOODBRIDES

NAME	M	WS	BS	S	T	W	A	Ld	Sv
Hekatrix Bloodbride	8"	3+	3+	3	3	1	2	8	6+
Syren	8"	3+	3+	3	3	1	3	8	6+

This unit contains 1 Syren and 4 Hekatrix Bloodbrides. It can include up to 5 additional Hekatrix Bloodbrides (**Power Rating +3**), up to 10 additional Hekatrix Bloodbrides (**Power Rating +6**), or up to 15 additional Hekatrix Bloodbrides (**Power Rating +9**). Each model is equipped with a splinter pistol, Hekatarii blade, and darklight grenades.

WEAPON	RANGE	TYPE	S	AP	D	ABILITIES
Blast pistol	6"	Pistol 1	8	-4	D3	-
Phantasm grenade launcher	18"	Assault D3	1	0	1	If a unit is hit by one or more phantasm grenade launchers, subtract one from its Leadership until the end of the turn.
Splinter pistol	12"	Pistol 1	*	0	1	This weapon wounds on a 4+, unless it is targeting a **VEHICLE**, in which case it wounds on a 6+.
Agoniser	Melee	Melee	*	-2	1	This weapon wounds on a 4+, unless it is targeting a **VEHICLE**, in which case it wounds on a 6+.
Hekatarii blade	Melee	Melee	User	0	1	Each time the bearer fights, it can make 1 additional attack with this weapon.
Hydra gauntlets	Melee	Melee	User	-1	1	Each time the bearer fights, it can make 1 additional attack with this weapon. You can re-roll failed wound rolls for this weapon.
Power sword	Melee	Melee	User	-3	1	-
Razorflails	Melee	Melee	User	-1	1	Each time the bearer fights, it can make 1 additional attack with this weapon. You can re-roll failed hit rolls for this weapon.
Shardnet and impaler	Melee	Melee	User	-1	2	-
Darklight grenade	6"	Grenade D6	4	-1	1	-

WARGEAR OPTIONS	• The Syren may take a phantasm grenade launcher. • The Syren may replace their splinter pistol with a blast pistol. • The Syren may replace their Hekatarii blade with a power sword or an agoniser. • One Bloodbride may replace their splinter pistol and Hekatarii blade with either razorflails, hydra gauntlets, or a shardnet and impaler. If the unit numbers 10 or more models, up to two further Bloodbrides may also do this.

ABILITIES	**Power From Pain, Combat Drugs** (pg 42) **Dodge:** Models in this unit have a 4+ invulnerable save in the Fight phase.	**No Escape:** Roll off if an enemy **INFANTRY** unit within 1" of any models with this ability wishes to Fall Back. The enemy unit can only Fall Back if the player commanding it wins the roll-off.

FACTION KEYWORDS	**AELDARI, DRUKHARI, <WYCH CULT>**
KEYWORDS	**INFANTRY, HEKATRIX BLOODBRIDES**

INCUBI

NAME	M	WS	BS	S	T	W	A	Ld	Sv
Incubi	7"	3+	3+	3	3	1	3	8	3+
Klaivex	7"	2+	3+	3	3	2	4	9	3+

This unit contains 1 Klaivex and 4 Incubi. It can include up to 5 additional Incubi (**Power Rating +4**). Each model is equipped with a klaive.

WEAPON	RANGE	TYPE	S	AP	D	ABILITIES
Demiklaives	Each time this model fights, choose one of the profiles below.					
- Single blade	Melee	Melee	+1	-3	1	-
- Dual blades	Melee	Melee	User	-2	1	A model attacking with dual blades can make 2 additional attacks with them each time it fights.
Klaive	Melee	Melee	+1	-3	1	-

WARGEAR OPTIONS	• The Klaivex may replace their klaive with demiklaives.
ABILITIES	**Power From Pain** (pg 42) **Lethal Precision:** Add 2 to the Damage characteristic of a close combat attack made by a Klaivex if the wound roll for the attack is 6+.
FACTION KEYWORDS	**AELDARI, DRUKHARI, INCUBI**
KEYWORDS	**INFANTRY**

MANDRAKES

NAME	M	WS	BS	S	T	W	A	Ld	Sv
Mandrake	8"	3+	3+	4	3	1	2	7	7+
Nightfiend	8"	3+	3+	4	3	1	3	8	7+

This unit contains 1 Nightfiend and 4 Mandrakes. It can include up to 5 additional Mandrakes (**Power Rating +4**). Each model is equipped with a baleblast and a glimmersteel blade.

WEAPON	RANGE	TYPE	S	AP	D	ABILITIES
Baleblast	18"	Assault 2	4	-1	1	Each time you roll a wound roll of 6+ for this weapon, the target suffers a mortal wound in addition to any other damage.
Glimmersteel blade	Melee	Melee	User	0	1	Each time the bearer fights, it can make 1 additional attack with this weapon.

ABILITIES	**Power From Pain** (pg 42) **From Out of the Shadows:** During deployment, you can set up this unit in the realm of Aelindrach instead of placing it on the battlefield. At the end of any of your Movement phases the Mandrakes can pull themselves into reality – set this unit up anywhere on the battlefield that is more than 9" away from any enemy models.	**Shrouded From Sight:** Your opponent must subtract 1 from the hit rolls of any attacks that target this unit. In addition, models in this unit have a 5+ invulnerable save.
FACTION KEYWORDS	**AELDARI, DRUKHARI**	
KEYWORDS	**INFANTRY, MANDRAKES**	

WRACKS

3 POWER

NAME	M	WS	BS	S	T	W	A	Ld	Sv
Wrack	7"	3+	3+	3	4	1	2	7	6+
Acothyst	7"	3+	3+	3	4	1	3	8	6+

This unit contains 1 Acothyst and 4 Wracks. It can include up to 5 additional Wracks (**Power Rating +3**). Each model is armed with Haemonculus tools.

WEAPON	RANGE	TYPE	S	AP	D	ABILITIES
Liquifier gun	8"	Assault D6	3	-D3	1	Each time this weapon is fired, roll a D3 to determine its AP for those attacks. For example, if you rolled a 1, this weapon would have an AP of -1. This weapon automatically hits its target.
Ossefactor	24"	Assault 1	*	-3	1	This weapon wounds on a 2+, unless it is targeting a **VEHICLE**, in which case it wounds on a 6+. If a model is slain by this weapon, the model's unit immediately suffers a mortal wound on a D6 roll of 4+.
Haemonculus tools	Melee	Melee	*	0	1	This weapon wounds on a 4+, unless it is targeting a **VEHICLE**, in which case it wounds on a 6+.

WARGEAR OPTIONS	• For every five models in the unit, one Wrack may take either a liquifier gun or ossefactor. • The Acothyst may take items from the *Weapons of Torture* and/or *Tools of Torment* lists.
ABILITIES	**Power From Pain** (pg 42) **Insensible To Pain:** Models in this unit have a 5+ invulnerable save.
FACTION KEYWORDS	AELDARI, DRUKHARI, <HAEMONCULUS COVEN>
KEYWORDS	INFANTRY, WRACKS

GROTESQUES

6 POWER

NAME	M	WS	BS	S	T	W	A	Ld	Sv
Grotesque	7"	3+	6+	5	5	3	4	8	6+

This unit contains 3 Grotesques. It can include up to 7 additional Grotesques (**Power Rating +2 per model**). Each model is armed with a monstrous cleaver and a flesh gauntlet.

WEAPON	RANGE	TYPE	S	AP	D	ABILITIES
Liquifier gun	8"	Assault D6	3	-D3	1	Each time this weapon is fired, roll a D3 to determine its AP for those attacks. For example, if you rolled a 1, this weapon would have an AP of -1. This weapon automatically hits its target.
Flesh gauntlet	Melee	Melee	*	0	1	This weapon wounds on a 4+, unless it is targeting a **VEHICLE**, in which case it wounds on a 6+. Each time you roll a wound roll of 6+ for this weapon, other than against **VEHICLES**, the target suffers a mortal wound in addition to any other damage.
Monstrous cleaver	Melee	Melee	User	-1	1	Each time the bearer fights, it can make 1 additional attack with this weapon.

WARGEAR OPTIONS	• Any model may replace its monstrous cleaver with a liquifier gun. • One Grotesque may take items from the *Weapons of Torture* list.
ABILITIES	**Power From Pain** (pg 42) **Insensible To Pain:** Models in this unit have a 5+ invulnerable save.
FACTION KEYWORDS	AELDARI, DRUKHARI, <HAEMONCULUS COVEN>
KEYWORDS	INFANTRY, GROTESQUES

BEASTMASTER

3 POWER

NAME	M	WS	BS	S	T	W	A	Ld	Sv
Beastmaster	12"	3+	3+	3	3	3	3	7	5+

A Beastmaster is a single model armed and a Beastmaster's scourge. It rides a skyboard equipped with splinter pods.

WEAPON	RANGE	TYPE	S	AP	D	ABILITIES
Splinter pods	18"	Assault 2	*	0	1	This weapon wounds on a 4+, unless it is targeting a Vehicle, in which case it wounds on a 6+.
Agoniser	Melee	Melee	*	-2	1	This weapon wounds on a 4+, unless it is targeting a Vehicle, in which case it wounds on a 6+.
Beastmaster's scourge	Melee	Melee	+1	0	1	-
Power sword	Melee	Melee	User	-3	1	-

WARGEAR OPTIONS	• This model may replace its Beastmaster's scourge with an agoniser or a power sword.
ABILITIES	**Power From Pain, Combat Drugs** (pg 42) **Beastmaster:** All friendly **DRUKHARI BEAST** units that are within 6" of a Beastmaster in the Fight phase can re-roll hit rolls, and all friendly **DRUKHARI BEAST** units that are within 6" of a Beastmaster in the Morale phase use the Beastmaster's Leadership instead of their own. In addition, if your army is Battle-forged, then for each Beastmaster in your army you can take a **DRUKHARI BEAST** unit in the same Detachment without taking up any of the Detachment's slots.
FACTION KEYWORDS	**AELDARI, DRUKHARI, <WYCH CULT>**
KEYWORDS	**CHARACTER, INFANTRY, FLY, BEASTMASTER**

CLAWED FIENDS

2 POWER

NAME	M	WS	BS	S	T	W	A	Ld	Sv
Clawed Fiend	10"	4+	-	5	5	4	5	4	5+

This unit contains 1 Clawed Fiend. It may include up to 2 additional Clawed Fiends (**Power Rating +3**) or up to 5 additional Clawed Fiends (**Power Rating +8**). Each model attacks with bludgeoning fists.

WEAPON	RANGE	TYPE	S	AP	D	ABILITIES
Bludgeoning fists	Melee	Melee	User	-1	2	-

FACTION KEYWORDS	**AELDARI, DRUKHARI**
KEYWORDS	**BEAST, CLAWED FIENDS**

KHYMERAE

1 POWER

NAME	M	WS	BS	S	T	W	A	Ld	Sv
Khymera	10"	3+	-	4	4	1	3	4	6+

This unit contains 2 Khymerae. It may include up to 5 additional pairs of Khymerae (**Power Rating +1 per pair**). Each model attacks with claws and talons.

WEAPON	RANGE	TYPE	S	AP	D	ABILITIES
Claws and talons	Melee	Melee	User	0	1	-

ABILITIES	**Otherworldly:** Models in this unit have a 5+ invulnerable save.
FACTION KEYWORDS	**AELDARI, DRUKHARI**
KEYWORDS	**BEAST, KHYMERAE**

RAZORWING FLOCKS

1 POWER

NAME	M	WS	BS	S	T	W	A	Ld	Sv
Razorwing Flock	12"	5+	-	2	2	4	8	4	7+

This unit contains up to 3 Razorwing Flocks. It may include up to 3 additional Razorwing Flocks (**Power Rating +1**) or up to 9 additional Razorwing Flocks (**Power Rating +3**). Each model is armed with claws and talons.

WEAPON	RANGE	TYPE	S	AP	D	ABILITIES
Claws and talons	Melee	Melee	User	0	1	-

FACTION KEYWORDS	AELDARI, DRUKHARI

KEYWORDS	BEAST, SWARM, FLY, RAZORWING FLOCKS

RAIDER

6 POWER

NAME	M	WS	BS	S	T	W	A	Ld	Sv
Raider	*	4+	*	6	5	10	*	7	4+

DAMAGE
Some of this model's characteristics change as it suffers damage, as shown below:

REMAINING W	M	BS	A
6-10+	14"	3+	3
3-5	10"	4+	D3
1-2	6"	5+	1

A Raider is a single model equipped with a dark lance and bladevanes.

WEAPON	RANGE	TYPE	S	AP	D	ABILITIES
Dark lance	36"	Heavy 1	8	-4	D6	Change the weapon's Type from Heavy to Assault if it is equipped on a **VEHICLE**.
Disintegrator cannon	36"	Assault 3	5	-3	2	-
Bladevanes	Melee	Melee	4	-1	1	-
Shock prow	Melee	Melee	User	-1	1	You can make a maximum of one close combat attack with a shock prow each turn (any remaining attacks must be made with a different melee weapon). If the bearer charged this turn, successful attacks with this weapon have a Damage characteristic of D3 instead of 1.

WARGEAR OPTIONS	• This model may replace its dark lance with a disintegrator cannon. • This model may take a shock prow.

ABILITIES	**Open-topped:** Models embarked on this model can attack in their Shooting phase. Measure the range and draw line of sight from any point on this model. When they do so, any restrictions or modifiers that apply to this model also apply to its passengers; for example, the passengers cannot shoot if this model has Fallen Back in the same turn, cannot shoot (except with Pistols) if this model is within 1" of an enemy unit, and so on. Note that the passengers cannot shoot if this model Falls Back, even though the Raider itself can.	**Night Shield:** This model has a 5+ invulnerable save against ranged weapons. **Explodes:** If this model is reduced to 0 wounds, roll a D6 before removing it from the battlefield and before any embarked models disembark. On a 6 it explodes, and each unit within 6" suffers D3 mortal wounds. **Hovering:** Distance and ranges are always measured to and from this model's hull, even though it has a base.

TRANSPORT	This model can transport 10 INCUBI or DRUKHARI INFANTRY models. Each Grotesque takes the space of two models.

FACTION KEYWORDS	AELDARI, DRUKHARI, <HAEMONCULUS COVEN> or <KABAL> or <WYCH CULT>

KEYWORDS	VEHICLE, TRANSPORT, FLY, RAIDER

VENOM

4 POWER

NAME	M	WS	BS	S	T	W	A	Ld	Sv
Venom	16"	4+	3+	5	5	6	2	7	4+

A Venom is a single model equipped with a twin splinter rifle, a splinter cannon and bladevanes.

WEAPON	RANGE	TYPE	S	AP	D	ABILITIES
Splinter cannon	36"	Rapid Fire 3	*	0	1	This weapon wounds on a 4+, unless it is targeting a **VEHICLE**, in which case it wounds on a 6+.
Twin splinter rifle	24"	Rapid Fire 2	*	0	1	This weapon wounds on a 4+, unless it is targeting a **VEHICLE**, in which case it wounds on a 6+.
Bladevanes	Melee	Melee	4	-1	1	-

WARGEAR OPTIONS	• This model may replace its twin splinter rifle with an additional splinter cannon.
ABILITIES	**Open-topped:** Models embarked on this model can attack in their Shooting phase. Measure the range and draw line of sight from any point on this model. When they do so, any restrictions or modifiers that apply to this model also apply to its passengers; for example, the passengers cannot shoot if this model has Fallen Back in the same turn, cannot shoot (except with Pistols) if this model is within 1" of an enemy unit, and so on. Note that the passengers cannot shoot if this model Falls Back, even though the Venom itself can. **Flickerfield:** Your opponent must subtract 1 from all hit rolls that target this model in the Shooting phase. **Explodes:** If this model is reduced to 0 wounds, roll a D6 before removing it from the battlefield and before any embarked models disembark. On a 6 it explodes, and each unit within 6" suffers 1 mortal wound. **Night Shield:** This model has a 5+ invulnerable save against ranged weapons.
TRANSPORT	This model can transport 5 **INCUBI** or **DRUKHARI INFANTRY** models, other than Grotesques.
FACTION KEYWORDS	**AELDARI, DRUKHARI, <HAEMONCULUS COVEN>** or **<KABAL>** or **<WYCH CULT>**
KEYWORDS	**VEHICLE, TRANSPORT, FLY, VENOM**

A Venom streaks into battle, its eager passengers ready for the slaughter.

REAVERS

NAME	M	WS	BS	S	T	W	A	Ld	Sv
Reaver	16"	3+	3+	3	4	2	2	7	4+
Arena Champion	16"	3+	3+	3	4	2	3	8	4+

This unit contains 1 Arena Champion and 2 Reavers. It can include up to 3 additional Reavers (**Power Rating +5**), up to 6 additional Reavers (**Power Rating +10**) or up to 9 additional Reavers (**Power Rating +15**). Each model is armed with a splinter pistol and rides a Reaver jetbike equipped with a splinter rifle and bladevanes.

WEAPON	RANGE	TYPE	S	AP	D	ABILITIES
Blaster	18"	Assault 1	8	-4	D3	-
Heat lance	18"	Assault 1	6	-5	D6	If the target is within half range of this weapon, roll two dice when inflicting damage with it and discard the lowest result.
Splinter pistol	12"	Pistol 1	*	0	1	This weapon wounds on a 4+, unless it is targeting a **Vehicle**, in which case it wounds on a 6+.
Splinter rifle	24"	Rapid Fire 1	*	0	1	This weapon wounds on a 4+, unless it is targeting a **Vehicle**, in which case it wounds on a 6+.
Agoniser	Melee	Melee	*	-2	1	This weapon wounds on a 4+, unless it is targeting a **Vehicle**, in which case it wounds on a 6+.
Bladevanes	Melee	Melee	4	-1	1	-
Power sword	Melee	Melee	User	-3	1	-

WARGEAR OPTIONS	
	• The Arena Champion may take either a power sword or an agoniser. • For every three models in the unit, one Reaver may replace its splinter rifle with a heat lance or blaster. • For every three models in the unit, one Reaver may take a grav-talon or cluster caltrops.

ABILITIES	
	Power From Pain, Combat Drugs (pg 42) **Cluster Caltrops:** Roll a D6 for each enemy unit within 1" of a model with cluster caltrops that Falls Back – on a 4+, that unit suffers a mortal wound.	**Grav-talon:** Roll a D6 each time a model with a grav-talon finishes a charge move within 1" of an enemy unit – on a 4+, that unit suffers a mortal wound. **Matchless Swiftness:** When this unit Advances, add 8" to its Move characteristic for that Movement phase instead of rolling a dice.

FACTION KEYWORDS	**Aeldari, Drukhari, <Wych Cult>**
KEYWORDS	**Biker, Fly, Reavers**

Piloted by the champions of the Commorrite arenas, Reaver jetbikes wreak havoc across the battlefield.

HELLIONS

NAME	M	WS	BS	S	T	W	A	Ld	Sv
Hellion	14"	3+	3+	3	3	1	2	7	5+
Helliarch	14"	3+	3+	3	3	1	3	8	5+

This unit contains 1 Helliarch and 4 Hellions. It can include up to 5 additional Hellions (**Power Rating +4**), up to 10 additional Hellions (**Power Rating +8**) or up to 15 additional Hellions (**Power Rating +12**). Each model is armed with splinter pods and a hellglaive.

WEAPON	RANGE	TYPE	S	AP	D	ABILITIES
Phantasm grenade launcher	18"	Assault D3	1	0	1	If a unit is hit by one or more phantasm grenade launchers, subtract one from its Leadership until the end of the turn.
Splinter pistol	12"	Pistol 1	*	0	1	This weapon wounds on a 4+, unless it is targeting a **Vehicle**, in which case it wounds on a 6+.
Splinter pods	18"	Assault 2	*	0	1	This weapon wounds on a 4+, unless it is targeting a **Vehicle**, in which case it wounds on a 6+.
Agoniser	Melee	Melee	*	-2	1	This weapon wounds on a 4+, unless it is targeting a **Vehicle**, in which case it wounds on a 6+.
Hellglaive	Melee	Melee	+1	0	2	-
Power sword	Melee	Melee	User	-3	1	-
Stunclaw	Melee	Melee	+1	0	1	Each time you roll a wound roll of 6+ for this weapon, the target suffers a mortal wound in addition to any other damage.

WARGEAR OPTIONS	
	• The Helliarch may take a phantasm grenade launcher.
	• The Helliarch may replace their hellglaive with one of the following options:
	- Splinter pistol and stunclaw
	- Splinter pistol and power sword
	- Splinter pistol and agoniser

ABILITIES	
	Power From Pain, Combat Drugs (pg 42)
	Hit and Run: If this unit Falls Back it can charge in the same turn.

FACTION KEYWORDS	**Aeldari, Drukhari, <Wych Cult>**
KEYWORDS	**Infantry, Fly, Hellions**

Hellion Gangs whoop with glee as they descend upon their foes in bladed flocks.

RAZORWING JETFIGHTER

8 POWER

NAME	M	WS	BS	S	T	W	A	Ld	Sv
Razorwing Jetfighter	*	6+	*	6	6	10	*	7	4+

DAMAGE
Some of this model's characteristics change as it suffers damage, as shown below:

REMAINING W	M	BS	A
6-10+	20-72"	3+	3
3-5	20-48"	4+	D3
1-2	20-32"	5+	1

A Razorwing Jetfighter is a single model equipped with two disintegrator cannons, a twin splinter rifle and Razorwing missiles.

WEAPON	RANGE	TYPE	S	AP	D	ABILITIES
Dark lance	36"	Heavy 1	8	-4	D6	Change the weapon's Type from Heavy to Assault if it is equipped on a **Vehicle**.
Disintegrator cannon	36"	Assault 3	5	-3	2	-
Razorwing missiles	When attacking with this weapon, choose one of the profiles below.					
- Monoscythe missile	48"	Assault D6	6	0	2	-
- Necrotoxin missile	48"	Assault 6	*	0	1	When you use this profile, this weapon wounds on a 2+, unless it is targeting a **Vehicle**, in which case it wounds on a 6+.
- Shatterfield missile	48"	Assault D6	7	-1	1	When you use this profile, you can re-roll failed wound rolls for this weapon.
Splinter cannon	36"	Rapid Fire 3	*	0	1	This weapon wounds on a 4+, unless it is targeting a **Vehicle**, in which case it wounds on a 6+.
Twin splinter rifle	24"	Rapid Fire 2	*	0	1	This weapon wounds on a 4+, unless it is targeting a **Vehicle**, in which case it wounds on a 6+.

WARGEAR OPTIONS	• This model may replace its two disintegrator cannons with two dark lances. • This model may replace its twin splinter rifle with a splinter cannon.

ABILITIES	**Supersonic:** Each time this model moves, first pivot it on the spot up to 90° (this does not contribute to how far the model moves), and then move the model straight forwards. Note that it cannot pivot again after the initial pivot. When this model Advances, increase its Move characteristic by 20" until the end of the phase – do not roll a dice. **Night Shield:** This model has a 5+ invulnerable save against ranged weapons.	**Hard to Hit:** Your opponent must subtract 1 from hit rolls for attacks that target this model in the Shooting phase. **Airborne:** This model cannot charge, can only be charged by units that can **Fly**, and can only attack or be attacked in the Fight phase by units that can **Fly**. **Crash and Burn:** If this model is reduced to 0 wounds, roll a D6 before removing it from the battlefield. On a 6 it crashes in a fiery explosion and each unit within 6" suffers D3 mortal wounds.

FACTION KEYWORDS	**Aeldari, Drukhari, <Kabal>** or **<Wych Cult>**
KEYWORDS	**Vehicle, Fly, Razorwing Jetfighter**

Razorwing Jetfighters scream over the battlefield, raining murder on the enemy below.

VOIDRAVEN

9 POWER

NAME	M	WS	BS	S	T	W	A	Ld	Sv
Voidraven	*	6+	*	6	6	12	*	7	4+

A Voidraven is a single model equipped with two void lances.

DAMAGE

Some of this model's characteristics change as it suffers damage, as shown below:

REMAINING W	M	BS	A
7-12+	20-60"	3+	3
4-6	20-40"	4+	D3
1-3	20-25"	5+	1

WEAPON	RANGE	TYPE	S	AP	D	ABILITIES
Dark scythe	24"	Assault D3	8	-4	D3	-
Void lance	36"	Assault 1	9	-4	D6	-
Voidraven missiles	When attacking with this weapon, choose one of the profiles below.					
- Implosion missile	48"	Assault D3	6	-3	1	-
- Shatterfield missile	48"	Assault D6	7	-1	1	You can re-roll failed wound rolls for this weapon.

WARGEAR OPTIONS
• This model may replace its two void lances with two dark scythes.
• This model may take Voidraven missiles.

ABILITIES

Crash and Burn: If this model is reduced to 0 wounds, roll a D6 before removing it from the battlefield. On a 6 it crashes in a fiery explosion and each unit within 6" suffers D3 mortal wounds.

Hard to Hit: Your opponent must subtract 1 from hit rolls for attacks that target this model in the Shooting phase.

Airborne: This model cannot charge, can only be charged by units that can **FLY**, and can only attack or be attacked in the Fight phase by units that can **FLY**.

Night Shield: This model has a 5+ invulnerable save against ranged weapons.

Supersonic: Each time this model moves, first pivot it on the spot up to 90° (this does not contribute to how far the model moves), and then move the model straight forwards. Note that it cannot pivot again after the initial pivot. When this model Advances, increase its Move characteristic by 20" until the end of the phase – do not roll a dice.

Void Mine: Once per battle, a Voidraven can drop a void mine on an enemy unit it moves over in one of its Movement phases. After the Voidraven has moved, pick one enemy unit that it flew over. Then, roll three D6 for each **VEHICLE** or **MONSTER** in the unit, or one D6 for every other model in the unit, up to a maximum of 10 D6. For each roll of 3+, the unit being bombed suffers a mortal wound.

FACTION KEYWORDS	AELDARI, DRUKHARI, <KABAL> or <WYCH CULT>
KEYWORDS	VEHICLE, FLY, VOIDRAVEN

Virtually invisible until they strike, Voidravens can obliterate swathes of the enemy with their lethal payloads.

SCOURGES

NAME	M	WS	BS	S	T	W	A	Ld	Sv
Scourge	14"	3+	3+	3	3	1	1	7	4+
Solarite	14"	3+	3+	3	3	1	2	8	4+

This unit contains 1 Solarite and 4 Scourges. It can include up to 5 additional Scourges (**Power Rating +4**). Each model is equipped with a shardcarbine and darklight grenades.

WEAPON	RANGE	TYPE	S	AP	D	ABILITIES
Blast pistol	6"	Pistol 1	8	-4	D3	-
Blaster	18"	Assault 1	8	-4	D3	-
Dark lance	36"	Heavy 1	8	-4	D6	-
Haywire blaster	24"	Assault 1	4	-1	1	If the target is a **VEHICLE** and you roll a wound roll of 4+ for this weapon, the target suffers a mortal wound in addition to any other damage. If the wound roll is 6+, inflict D3 mortal wounds instead of 1.
Heat lance	18"	Assault 1	6	-5	D6	If the target is within half range of this weapon, roll two dice when inflicting damage with it and discard the lowest result.
Shardcarbine	18"	Assault 3	*	0	1	This weapon wounds on a 4+, unless it is targeting a **VEHICLE**, in which case it wounds on a 6+.
Shredder	12"	Assault D3	6	0	1	When attacking a unit of **INFANTRY**, you can re-roll failed wound rolls for this weapon.
Splinter cannon	36"	Rapid Fire 3	*	0	1	This weapon wounds on a 4+, unless it is targeting a **VEHICLE**, in which case it wounds on a 6+.
Splinter pistol	12"	Pistol 1	*	0	1	This weapon wounds on a 4+, unless it is targeting a **VEHICLE**, in which case it wounds on a 6+.
Agoniser	Melee	Melee	*	-2	1	This weapon wounds on a 4+, unless it is targeting a **VEHICLE**, in which case it wounds on a 6+.
Power lance	Melee	Melee	+2	-1	1	-
Venom blade	Melee	Melee	*	0	1	This weapon wounds on a 2+, unless it is targeting a **VEHICLE**, in which case it wounds on a 6+.
Darklight grenade	6"	Grenade D6	4	-1	1	-

WARGEAR OPTIONS	• Up to four Scourges may replace their shardcarbine with either a splinter cannon, dark lance, heat lance, shredder, haywire blaster or blaster. • The Solarite may replace their shardcarbine with either a splinter pistol or blast pistol. • If the Solarite replaces their shardcarbine with a pistol they may also take a venom blade, power lance or agoniser.

ABILITIES	**Power From Pain** (pg 42) **Ghostplate Armour:** Models in this unit have a 6+ invulnerable save.	**Winged Strike:** During deployment, you can set up a Scourge unit flying high in the skies instead of placing it on the battlefield. At the end of any of your Movement phases the Scourge unit can use a winged strike to arrive – set them up anywhere on the battlefield that is more than 9" away from any enemy models.

FACTION KEYWORDS	**AELDARI, DRUKHARI**
KEYWORDS	**INFANTRY, FLY, SCOURGES**

TALOS

NAME	M	WS	BS	S	T	W	A	Ld	Sv
Talos	8"	3+	4+	6	6	7	4	8	3+

This unit contains 1 Talos. It may contain an additional Talos (**Power Rating +7**) or 2 additional Talos (**Power Rating +14**). Each model is equipped with two splinter cannons and two macro-scalpels.

WEAPON	RANGE	TYPE	S	AP	D	ABILITIES
Haywire blaster	24"	Assault 1	4	-1	1	If the target is a **Vehicle** and you roll a wound roll of 4+ for this weapon, the target suffers 1 mortal wound in addition to any other damage. If the wound roll is 6+, inflict D3 mortal wounds instead of 1.
Heat lance	18"	Assault 1	6	-5	D6	If the target is within half range of this weapon, roll two dice when inflicting damage with it and discard the lowest result.
Splinter cannon	36"	Rapid Fire 3	*	0	1	This weapon wounds on a 4+, unless it is targeting a **Vehicle**, in which case it wounds on a 6+.
Stinger pod	24"	Assault 2D6	5	0	1	-
Twin liquifier gun	8"	Assault 2D6	3	-D3	1	Each time this weapon is fired, roll a D3 to determine its AP for those attacks. For example, if you rolled a 1, this weapon would have an AP of -1. This weapon automatically hits its target.
Chain-flails	Melee	Melee	User	0	1	You can re-roll failed wound rolls for this weapon.
Ichor injector	Melee	Melee	User	0	1	The bearer can make a maximum of one attack with the ichor injector each turn (any remaining attacks must be made with a different melee weapon). You can re-roll wound rolls for this weapon. Each time you roll a wound roll of 6+ for this weapon, the target suffers D3 mortal wounds in addition to any other damage.
Macro-scalpel	Melee	Melee	User	-1	2	A model armed with a macro-scalpel can make one additional close combat attack with it each time it fights. A model armed with two macro-scalpels can make two additional close combat attacks with them each time it fights.

WARGEAR OPTIONS	• Any Talos may replace one of its macro-scalpels with chain-flails, an ichor injector or a twin liquifier gun. • Any Talos may replace its two splinter cannons with a stinger pod, two heat lances or two haywire blasters.
ABILITIES	**Power From Pain** (pg 42) **Insensible To Pain:** Models in this unit have a 5+ invulnerable save. **Explodes:** If this model is reduced to 0 wounds, roll a D6 before removing it from the battlefield. On a 6 it explodes, and each unit within 6" suffers a mortal wound.
FACTION KEYWORDS	**Aeldari, Drukhari, <Haemonculus Coven>**
KEYWORDS	**Monster, Talos**

CRONOS

NAME	M	WS	BS	S	T	W	A	Ld	Sv
Cronos	8"	4+	4+	5	6	7	3	9	3+

This unit contains 1 Cronos. It may contain an additional Cronos (**Power Rating +5**) or 2 additional Cronos (**Power Rating +10**). Each model is equipped with a spirit syphon and spirit-leech tentacles.

WEAPON	RANGE	TYPE	S	AP	D	ABILITIES
Spirit syphon	8"	Assault D6	3	-2	1	This weapon automatically hits its target. Any attacks with a wound roll of 6+ for this weapon have a Damage characteristic of D3 instead of 1.
Spirit vortex	18"	Assault D6	3	-2	1	Any attacks with a wound roll of 6+ for this weapon have a Damage characteristic of D3 instead of 1.
Spirit-leech tentacles	Melee	Melee	User	-1	1	Any attacks with a wound roll of 6+ for this weapon have a Damage characteristic of D3 instead of 1.

WARGEAR OPTIONS	• Any model may take a spirit vortex.

ABILITIES	Power From Pain (pg 42) **Insensible To Pain:** Models in this unit have a 5+ invulnerable save. **Explodes:** If this model is reduced to 0 wounds, roll a D6 before removing it from the battlefield. On a 6 it explodes, and each unit within 6" suffers a mortal wound.	**Spirit Probe:** You can re-roll wound rolls of 1 for friendly **DRUKHARI** units that are within 6" of this model in the Fight phase. In addition, if a Cronos inflicts one or more wounds in the Fight phase, you can pick a friendly **DRUKHARI** unit within 6" of the Cronos that is not a **VEHICLE**. The unit you pick recovers 1 wound lost earlier in the battle.

FACTION KEYWORDS	AELDARI, DRUKHARI, <HAEMONCULUS COVEN>
KEYWORDS	MONSTER, CRONOS

RAVAGER

DAMAGE
Some of this model's characteristics change as it suffers damage, as shown below:

REMAINING W	M	BS	A
6-10+	14"	3+	3
3-5	10"	4+	D3
1-2	6"	5+	1

NAME	M	WS	BS	S	T	W	A	Ld	Sv
Ravager	✱	4+	✱	6	6	10	✱	7	4+

A Ravager is a single model equipped with bladevanes and three dark lances.

WEAPON	RANGE	TYPE	S	AP	D	ABILITIES
Dark lance	36"	Heavy 1	8	-4	D6	Change the weapon's Type from Heavy to Assault if it is equipped on a **VEHICLE**.
Disintegrator cannon	36"	Assault 3	5	-3	2	-
Bladevanes	Melee	Melee	4	-1	1	-
Shock prow	Melee	Melee	User	-1	1	You can make a maximum of one close combat attack with a shock prow each turn (any remaining attacks must be made with a different melee weapon). If the bearer charged this turn, successful attacks with this weapon have a Damage characteristic of D3 instead of 1.

WARGEAR OPTIONS	• This model may replace any of its dark lances with a disintegrator cannon. • This model may take a shock prow.

ABILITIES	**Night Shield:** This model has a 5+ invulnerable save. **Explodes:** If this model is reduced to 0 wounds, roll a D6 before removing it from the battlefield. On a 6 it explodes, and each unit within 6" suffers D3 mortal wounds.

FACTION KEYWORDS	AELDARI, DRUKHARI, <KABAL>
KEYWORDS	VEHICLE, FLY, RAVAGER

The Haemonculus Covens spearhead the Drukhari attack in a tide of gruesome horrors and flesh-twisted fiends.

HARLEQUINS

To the warrior-acrobats of the Harlequins, warfare and art are inseparable disciplines. These mysterious nomads travel between the realms of their divided race, fighting a never-ending war against Chaos on behalf of their Laughing God even as they seek to rekindle the glory of the ancient Aeldari.

When the Aeldari empire fell and Slaanesh was birthed from the roiling seas of the warp, almost the entirety of the Aeldari pantheon was devoured by She Who Thirsts. Only one deity escaped – Cegorach, the Laughing God. Ever the most cunning and elusive of his kind, Cegorach hid amongst the myriad passages of the webway while Slaanesh slew his brother and sister gods. The legends say that he dwells there still, plotting vengeful schemes against the Dark Powers. Many of Cegorach's followers fled alongside him, hiding in the depths of that transdimensional labyrinth and thus evading the hunger of the nascent Chaos God. There they lived for millennia, all the while waging a clandestine war against She Who Thirsts on behalf of their trickster patron. As the galaxy grows ever darker, more and more Aeldari disappear into the webway to take up the mask of the Harlequin. They leave their sacred spirit stones behind, for the Laughing God's followers possess the secret of avoiding Slaanesh's eternal hunger.

Enigmatic and mercurial, the Harlequins of Cegorach remain a mystery even to their Aeldari cousins. They are tricksters and mummers as much as they are warriors, though one should not be deceived by the colourful motley they wear – Harlequins fight with bewildering speed and masterful skill, laughing with dark humour even as they slice their opponents to ribbons. When assembled into the travelling companies known as masques, Harlequins make war with an almost prescient cohesion, each individual player performing his role with skill born from countless centuries of practice.

Daemonic threats beyond counting have been destroyed or subverted by these enigmatic beings, and the populations of entire sectors saved without ever knowing they were in danger. The Harlequins strike from webway gates with blinding speed, killing their targets with masterful skill and precision before vanishing as swiftly as they arrived. Alongside these martial endeavours, Harlequins perform another, more sacred duty: they travel amongst the scattered factions of their race, performing the dances and plays of the Aeldari mythic cycle. Their audiences view these ritual performances with great reverence, for they are a tangible link to the past, a reminder of the Aeldari's noble origins. In this way, the Harlequins ensure a modicum of racial unity still exists between Exodites, Craftworld Aeldari, and even the Drukhari of the Dark City. Indeed, in times of great strife they sow the seeds of temporary alliances between their fractured kin.

HARLEQUIN MASQUES

The Harlequin masques are both armies and companies of players. They have no formal leaders, and instead operate as a disciplined ensemble, each individual role within the company as important as any other. The masques are centred around three distinct Troupes; the Light, the Dark and the Twilight, each with its own outlook and symbolism. Each member of the Troupe is assigned his or her own role to play – characters include the Webway Witch, the Sun Prince, or Shaimesh the Poisoner – and assumes this personality from then on, both in battle and upon the stage. This structure ensures that a masque fights with astonishing synchronicity and cohesion, for they have rehearsed for each battle hundreds of times before.

Further establishing the link between the Harlequins' dual roles as performers and warriors are the battlefield strategies known as *saedath*, which take inspiration from the mythic plays that the masques perform. There is a saedath for each and every strategic situation, chosen depending on the foe, the battlefield, and countless other omens and factors. All are intricate and brilliantly conceived.

With impossible grace and poise the Troupes leap into battle, their holo-suits distorting their outlines into a fractal explosion of colour, their blades flickering out to pierce hearts and slice throats. Every step they take is a part of a dance that they have spent their entire lives mastering, and the screams of the dying enemy are their rapturous applause. Troupe Masters choreograph the slaughter, punctuating each beat with eloquent flourishes of violence. Death Jesters stalk through the chaos of battle, unleashing searing fusillades from their oversized weapons, adding an undercurrent of black humour to the masque's performance as they attempt to make their foes' demise as darkly comic as possible; severing the arm of a soldier wielding a primed grenade before he can throw it, or blasting the legs from underneath a corpulent Daemon so that he collapses upon his unfortunate underlings, crushing them beneath his blubbery weight.

Above the battlefield Skyweavers arc and roll, their holo-grenades erupting in a maddening tapestry of prismatic hues that tugs at the sanity of those who witness it. Larger grav-skimmers follow in their wake. Starweavers are named after the first son of the Cosmic Serpent, a totemic figure amongst the Harlequins whose offspring were once great allies of Cegorach. They are utilised as swift transports, though their shuriken cannons can also provide supporting fire for the Harlequins once they have leapt into the fray.

Voidweavers sacrifice this transport capacity for raw firepower. Named after the second of the Cosmic Serpent's brood – an ill-tempered and suspicious creature who sprouted a second head so that it would never be caught unaware by its foes – these sturdy vehicles bristle with shuriken and haywire cannons. An aft cannon spews a withering hail of fire at pursuing aircraft, a deadly tribute to its mythical namesake.

In the Harlequins' performances it is the Shadowseers who play the role of fate. They are the masque's narrators and storytellers, and by virtue of their psychic ability, and the hallucinogenic *creidann* grenade launchers they wear upon their backs, they also provide the illusory and pyrokinetic displays that accompany these grand shows. In battle, the Shadowseers turn these talents towards the obliteration of their enemies' minds, weaving illusion and fear around themselves like a psychic tempest. Foes gibber and scream as they hack at unseen horrors, or laugh so hard that their lungs rupture and fill with blood.

A blur of colour shifts through the enemy ranks, too fast for the eye to follow. In its wake, arcs of crimson spurt into the air, and warriors fall to the ground clutching helplessly at opened throats and slashed arteries. For a fraction of a second the Solitaire stops to observe the ruination he has left in his wake, his horned mask gazing at the twitching bodies of the dying dispassionately, before he leaps into the thick of combat once more. Solitaires are grim figures, forever isolated from those they fight alongside. In the story of the Fall they play the role of Slaanesh, the nemesis of all Aeldari, and thus they are seen as figures of doom and terror amongst their kin. Even their fellow Harlequins treat Solitaires with cautious respect, for these solemn killers tread the Path of Damnation alone, drifting between masques for a performance or battle before moving on once more. Unlike their fellow players, Solitaires are doomed to be devoured by She Who Thirsts, and this knowledge grants them a grim determination to cost their enemies dear before they meet their end.

The combination of these esoteric fighting styles may appear as little more than a chaotic riot of colour and violence to the untrained eye, but to the heightened senses of the Aeldari it is a thing of complex beauty. It is perfection of form, the apotheosis of war as art.

HARLEQUINS ARMY LIST

This section contains all of the datasheets that you will need in order to fight battles with your Harlequin miniatures. Each datasheet includes the characteristics profiles of the unit it describes, as well as any wargear and abilities it may have. The Rising Crescendo ability is common to several Harlequin units – it is described below and referenced on the datasheets.

ABILITIES

The following ability is common to several Harlequin units:

Rising Crescendo

Units with this ability can Advance and charge in the same turn. In addition, they can Fall Back and still shoot and/or charge in the same turn.

PHANTASMANCY DISCIPLINE

Before the battle, generate the psychic powers for **PSYKERS** that can use powers from the Phantasmancy discipline using the table below. You can either roll a D3 to generate their powers randomly (re-roll any duplicate results), or you can select the psychic powers you wish the psyker to have.

PHANTASMANCY DISCIPLINE	
D3	**PSYCHIC POWER**
1	**Twilight Pathways** *Twilight Pathways* has a warp charge value of 6. If manifested, select a visible friendly **HARLEQUINS** unit within 3" of the psyker. That unit can immediately move as if it were its Movement phase. You cannot use *Twilight Pathways* on a unit more than once in each Psychic phase.
2	**Fog of Dreams** *Fog of Dreams* has a warp charge value of 7. If manifested, select a visible enemy unit within 18" of the psyker. Until the start of your next Psychic phase, your opponent must subtract 1 from all hit rolls for that unit that target **HARLEQUIN INFANTRY** units.
3	**Mirror of Minds** *Mirror of Minds* has a warp charge value of 8. If manifested, select an enemy unit within 24" of the psyker. Then, both players roll a dice. If the Harlequin player's roll is equal to or higher than their opponent's, then the target unit suffers 1 mortal wound. Repeat this process until the target is destroyed, or the enemy player rolls a result that is higher than the Harlequin player's roll.

KEYWORDS

Throughout this section you will come across a keyword that is within angular brackets, specifically <**MASQUE**>. This is shorthand for a keyword of your own choosing, as described below.

<**MASQUE**>

Most Harlequins belong to a masque and have the <**MASQUE**> keyword. When you include such a unit in your army, you must nominate which masque that unit is from. You then simply replace the <**MASQUE**> keyword in every instance on that unit's datasheet with the name of your chosen masque.

For example, if you were to include a Troupe Master in your army, and you decided they were from the Midnight Sorrow masque, his <**MASQUE**> Faction keyword is changed to **MIDNIGHT SORROW** and his Choreographer of War ability would then say 'All friendly **MIDNIGHT SORROW** units that are within 6" of this model in the Fight phase can re-roll failed wound rolls.'

TROUPE

7 POWER

NAME	M	WS	BS	S	T	W	A	Ld	Sv
Player	8"	3+	3+	3	3	1	4	8	6+

This unit contains 5 Players. It can include up to 7 additional Players (**Power Rating +1 per model**). Each model is armed with a shuriken pistol, Harlequin's blade and prismatic grenades.

WEAPON	RANGE	TYPE	S	AP	D	ABILITIES
Fusion pistol	6"	Pistol 1	8	-4	D6	If the target is within half range of this weapon, roll two dice when inflicting damage with it and discard the lowest result.
Neuro disruptor	12"	Pistol 1	3	-3	D3	This weapon has a Damage of 1 against **VEHICLE** targets.
Shuriken pistol	12"	Pistol 1	4	0	1	Each time you make a wound roll of 6+ for this weapon, that hit is resolved with an AP of -3 instead of 0.
Harlequin's blade	Melee	Melee	User	0	1	-
Harlequin's caress	Melee	Melee	5	-2	1	-
Harlequin's embrace	Melee	Melee	4	-3	1	-
Harlequin's kiss	Melee	Melee	4	-1	D3	-
Prismatic grenade	6"	Grenade D6	4	-1	1	-

WARGEAR OPTIONS	• Any model may replace its shuriken pistol with a neuro disruptor or fusion pistol. • Any model may replace its Harlequin's blade with a Harlequin's embrace, Harlequin's kiss or Harlequin's caress.
ABILITIES	**Rising Crescendo** (pg 68) **Flip Belt:** This unit can move across models and terrain as if they were not there.	**Holo-suit:** Models in this unit have a 4+ invulnerable save.
FACTION KEYWORDS	**AELDARI, HARLEQUINS, <MASQUE>**
KEYWORDS	**INFANTRY, TROUPE**

Immersed in the roles they have played for centuries beyond counting, Harlequin Troupes fight with preternatural skill.

TROUPE MASTER

NAME	M	WS	BS	S	T	W	A	Ld	Sv
Troupe Master	8"	2+	2+	3	3	5	5	9	6+

A Troupe Master is a single model armed with a shuriken pistol, Harlequin's blade and prismatic grenades.

WEAPON	RANGE	TYPE	S	AP	D	ABILITIES
Fusion pistol	6"	Pistol 1	8	-4	D6	If the target is within half range of this weapon, roll two dice when inflicting damage with it and discard the lowest result.
Neuro disruptor	12"	Pistol 1	3	-3	D3	This weapon has a Damage of 1 against **VEHICLE** targets.
Shuriken pistol	12"	Pistol 1	4	0	1	Each time you make a wound roll of 6+ for this weapon, that hit is resolved with an AP of -3 instead of 0.
Harlequin's blade	Melee	Melee	User	0	1	-
Harlequin's caress	Melee	Melee	5	-2	1	-
Harlequin's embrace	Melee	Melee	4	-3	1	-
Harlequin's kiss	Melee	Melee	4	-1	D3	-
Power sword	Melee	Melee	User	-3	1	-
Prismatic grenade	6"	Grenade D6	4	-1	1	-

WARGEAR OPTIONS	• This model may replace its shuriken pistol with a neuro disruptor or fusion pistol. • This model may replace its Harlequin's blade with a power sword, Harlequin's embrace, Harlequin's kiss or Harlequin's caress.
ABILITIES	**Rising Crescendo** (pg 68) **Flip Belt:** This model can move across models and terrain as if they were not there. **Holo-suit:** This model has a 4+ invulnerable save.	**Choreographer of War:** All friendly **<MASQUE>** units that are within 6" of this model in the Fight phase can re-roll failed wound rolls.
FACTION KEYWORDS	**AELDARI, HARLEQUINS, <MASQUE>**
KEYWORDS	**CHARACTER, INFANTRY, TROUPE MASTER**

DEATH JESTER

NAME	M	WS	BS	S	T	W	A	Ld	Sv
Death Jester	8"	2+	2+	3	3	5	4	9	6+

A Death Jester is a single model armed with a shrieker cannon.

WEAPON	RANGE	TYPE	S	AP	D	ABILITIES
Shrieker cannon		When attacking with this weapon, choose one of the profiles below. Each time you make a wound roll of 6+ for this weapon, that hit is resolved with an AP of -3 instead of 0.				
- Shrieker	24"	Assault 1	6	0	1	If an **INFANTRY** model is slain by an attack made with this weapon, then its unit suffers D3 mortal wounds.
- Shuriken	24"	Assault 3	6	0	1	-

ABILITIES	**Rising Crescendo** (pg 68) **Deadly Hunter:** This model may target a **CHARACTER** even if it is not the closest enemy unit. **Death Is Not Enough:** If any models flee from a unit in the same turn that it has been attacked by this model, then you can choose the first model that flees instead of your opponent choosing.	**Flip Belt:** This model can move across models and terrain as if they were not there. **Holo-suit:** This model has a 4+ invulnerable save.
FACTION KEYWORDS	**AELDARI, HARLEQUINS, <MASQUE>**	
KEYWORDS	**CHARACTER, INFANTRY, DEATH JESTER**	

☠ (7) POWER — SHADOWSEER

NAME	M	WS	BS	S	T	W	A	Ld	Sv
Shadowseer	8"	2+	2+	3	3	5	3	9	7+

A Shadowseer is a single model armed with a shuriken pistol, a hallucinogen grenade launcher and a miststave.

WEAPON	RANGE	TYPE	S	AP	D	ABILITIES
Hallucinogen grenade launcher	18"	Assault 1	*	*	*	Roll 2D6 if a unit is hit by this weapon – if the roll is equal to or greater than the target unit's Leadership, then it suffers D3 mortal wounds.
Neuro disruptor	12"	Pistol 1	3	-3	D3	This weapon has a Damage of 1 against **VEHICLE** targets.
Shuriken pistol	12"	Pistol 1	4	0	1	Each time you make a wound roll of 6+ for this weapon, that hit is resolved with an AP of -3 instead of 0.
Miststave	Melee	Melee	+2	-1	D3	-

WARGEAR OPTIONS	• This model may replace its shuriken pistol with a neuro disruptor.

ABILITIES	**Rising Crescendo** (pg 68)	**Shield from Harm:** Your opponent must subtract 1 from the wound rolls for any attacks made against this model, and for attacks against any friendly **\<MASQUE\> INFANTRY** units that are within 6" of one or more models with this ability.
	Flip Belt: This model can move across models and terrain as if they were not there.	
	Holo-suit: This model has a 4+ invulnerable save.	

PSYKER	This model can attempt to manifest two psychic powers in each friendly Psychic phase, and attempt to deny one psychic power in each enemy Psychic phase. It knows the *Smite* power and one psychic power from the Phantasmancy discipline (pg 68).

FACTION KEYWORDS	AELDARI, HARLEQUINS, \<MASQUE\>
KEYWORDS	CHARACTER, INFANTRY, PSYKER, SHADOWSEER

✠ (6) POWER — SOLITAIRE

NAME	M	WS	BS	S	T	W	A	Ld	Sv
Solitaire	12"	2+	2+	3	3	5	8	9	6+

A Solitaire is a single model armed with a Harlequin's caress and a Harlequin's kiss. Only one of this model may be included in your army.

WEAPON	RANGE	TYPE	S	AP	D	ABILITIES
Harlequin's caress	Melee	Melee	5	-2	1	-
Harlequin's kiss	Melee	Melee	4	-1	D3	-

ABILITIES	**Rising Crescendo** (pg 68)	**Impossible Form:** The Solitaire has a 3+ invulnerable save.
	Blitz: Once per battle, instead of making a normal move with the Solitaire, you can make a Blitz move with it. If you do so, add 2D6" to the model's Move characteristic for this turn. In addition, the model's Attacks characteristic is increased to 10 for the rest of the turn. This ability may not be used if the model has been selected as the target of the *Twilight Pathways* psychic power in the previous Psychic phase.	**Flip Belt:** The Solitaire can move across models and terrain as if they were not there.

FACTION KEYWORDS	AELDARI, HARLEQUINS
KEYWORDS	CHARACTER, INFANTRY, SOLITAIRE

SKYWEAVERS

NAME	M	WS	BS	S	T	W	A	Ld	Sv
Skyweavers	16"	3+	3+	3	4	3	3	8	4+

This unit contains 2 Skyweavers. It can include up to 2 additional Skyweavers (**Power Rating +5**) or up to 4 additional Skyweavers (**Power Rating +10**). Each model is equipped with a shuriken cannon and star bolas.

WEAPON	RANGE	TYPE	S	AP	D	ABILITIES
Haywire cannon	24"	Heavy D3	4	-1	1	If the target is a **VEHICLE** and you roll a wound roll of 4+ for this weapon, the target suffers 1 mortal wound in addition to any other damage. If the wound roll is 6+, the target suffers D3 mortal wounds instead of 1.
Shuriken cannon	24"	Assault 3	6	0	1	Each time you make a wound roll of 6+ for this weapon, that hit is resolved with an AP of -3 instead of 0.
Zephyrglaive	Melee	Melee	+1	-2	2	-
Star bolas	12"	Grenade D3	6	-3	1	-

WARGEAR OPTIONS	• Any model may replace its star bolas with a zephyrglaive. • Any model may replace its shuriken cannon with a haywire cannon.	
ABILITIES	Rising Crescendo (pg 68) **Blur of Colour:** When this unit Advances, add 6" to its Move characteristic for that Movement phase instead of rolling a dice.	**Holo-suit:** Models in this unit have a 4+ invulnerable save. **Mirage Launchers:** Your opponent must subtract 1 from any hit rolls made against this unit in the Shooting phase.
FACTION KEYWORDS	**AELDARI, HARLEQUINS, <MASQUE>**	
KEYWORDS	**BIKER, FLY, SKYWEAVERS**	

STARWEAVER

NAME	M	WS	BS	S	T	W	A	Ld	Sv
Starweaver	16"	3+	3+	5	5	6	3	8	4+

A Starweaver is a single model armed with two shuriken cannons.

WEAPON	RANGE	TYPE	S	AP	D	ABILITIES
Shuriken cannon	24"	Assault 3	6	0	1	Each time you make a wound roll of 6+ for this weapon, that hit is resolved with an AP of -3 instead of 0.

ABILITIES	**Open-topped:** Models embarked on this model can attack in their Shooting phase. Measure the range and draw line of sight from any point on this model. When they do so, any restrictions or modifiers that apply to this model also apply to its passengers; for example, the passengers cannot shoot if this model has Fallen Back in the same turn, cannot shoot (except with Pistols) if this model is within 1" of an enemy unit, and so on. Note that the passengers cannot shoot if this model Falls Back, even though the Starweaver itself can. **Blur of Colour:** When this model Advances, add 6" to its Move characteristic for that Movement phase instead of rolling a dice.	**Holo-fields:** This model has a 4+ invulnerable save. **Mirage Launchers:** Your opponent must subtract 1 from any hit rolls made against this model in the Shooting phase. **Explodes:** If this model is reduced to 0 wounds, roll a D6 before removing it from the battlefield and before any models disembark. On a 6 it explodes, and each unit within 6" suffers 1 mortal wound.
TRANSPORT	A Starweaver can transport 6 <MASQUE> INFANTRY models.	
FACTION KEYWORDS	**AELDARI, HARLEQUINS, <MASQUE>**	
KEYWORDS	**VEHICLE, TRANSPORT, FLY, STARWEAVER**	

VOIDWEAVERS

NAME	M	WS	BS	S	T	W	A	Ld	Sv
Voidweaver	16"	3+	3+	5	5	6	3	8	4+

This unit contains 1 Voidweaver. It can include 1 additional Voidweaver (**Power Rating +6**) or 2 additional Voidweavers (**Power Rating +12**). Each model is equipped with two shuriken cannons and one haywire cannon.

WEAPON	RANGE	TYPE	S	AP	D	ABILITIES
Haywire cannon	24"	Heavy D3	4	-1	1	If the target is a **VEHICLE** and you roll a wound roll of 4+ for this weapon, the target suffers 1 mortal wound in addition to any other damage. If the wound roll is 6+, the target suffers D3 mortal wounds instead of 1.
Prismatic cannon		When attacking with this weapon, choose one of the profiles below.				
- Dispersed	24"	Heavy D6	4	-2	1	-
- Focused	24"	Heavy D3	6	-3	D3	-
- Lance	24"	Heavy 1	8	-4	D6	-
Shuriken cannon	24"	Assault 3	6	0	1	Each time you make a wound roll of 6+ for this weapon, that hit is resolved with an AP of -3 instead of 0.

WARGEAR OPTIONS	• Any model may replace its haywire cannon with a prismatic cannon.

ABILITIES	**Blur of Colour:** When this unit Advances, add 6" to its Move characteristic for that Movement phase instead of rolling a dice.
	Holo-fields: Models in this unit have a 4+ invulnerable save.
	Mirage Launchers: Your opponent must subtract 1 from any hit rolls made against this model in the Shooting phase.
	Explodes: If this model is reduced to 0 wounds, roll a D6 before removing it from the battlefield. On a 6 it explodes, and each unit within 6" suffers 1 mortal wound.

FACTION KEYWORDS	**AELDARI, HARLEQUINS, <MASQUE>**
KEYWORDS	**VEHICLE, FLY, VOIDWEAVERS**

Voidweavers knife through the air, their holo-fields and mirage launchers turning the battlefield into a kaleidoscopic nightmare.

YNNARI

The Ynnari, known as the Reborn, are a rising force in the galaxy. They believe the Aeldari can be saved from the brink of oblivion by the rise of Ynnead, the God of the Dead, whose powers they harness to draw upon the energies of the slain.

There is an obscure school of thought in Aeldari society that states when every Aeldari has died and passed into the infinity circuits of the craftworlds they will form a gestalt, awakening a new god with the power to end Slaanesh's baleful curse. Some seers and scholars claim that time of ending is nigh, but that not all Aeldari must die to escape Slaanesh's clutches – that there is a new hope to be found amongst the darkness. Foremost amongst these is Eldrad Ulthran, the High Farseer of Ulthwé, whose psychic machinations have led to a premature awakening for the Aeldari God of the Dead.

Soon after Ynnead was first roused from slumbering potentiality, a fraction of his will and power was imparted to Yvraine, the Daughter of Shades – chosen by fate, she was in spirit the closest living thing to the ancient Aeldari that had existed before Slaanesh erupted into being. Originally a Biel-Tani, Yvraine had journeyed to every corner of Aeldari society – she had become an Outcast, then a Corsair commander, and finally, after a costly mutiny, fallen from grace entirely to become exiled from even the most roguish of Aeldari sub-cultures. She eked out a new existence from the dark streets of Commorragh, fighting tooth and nail to become part of the Wych Cults – such was her skill as a warrior that she rose to the rank of Succubus. It was in the white-hot crucible of arena conflict that she crossed the threshold of death, and found herself infused with the energies of Ynnead. That was the crucial point of fate that saw the birth of a new creed – in one mind-blasting moment Yvraine became a conduit for deathly energies, invested with the ability to pass on her esoteric skills to those who joined her new and macabre religion.

With the aid of the mysterious swordsman known as the Visarch, Yvraine cut her way free from the daemonic infestation that rocked Commorragh soon after her ascension. She made her way back to the craftworld of her birth, ripping free one of the fabled Croneswords from the wraithbone skeleton of Biel-Tan – and in the process fracturing the world-ship into

shards of its former glory. The shattering of Biel-Tan's infinity circuit caused a vast explosion of psychic energies, spawning spiralling warp vortices around the stricken craftworld, but also giving a focal point for the Aeldari God of the Dead to manifest his avatar in realspace. So was born the Yncarne, a being both beautiful and terrible, whose mastery over deathly energies were the supernatural powers of Ynnead himself.

Since that fateful day the Triumvirate of Ynnead has spread word of the nascent god's ascension to the mightiest of craftworlds, the far-flung fleets of the Corsairs and even the dark and troubled spires of Commorragh. A great many Aeldari and Drukhari have joined their cause, hailing from every sub-faction and allegiance save the most conservative and entrenched. No abstract school of philosophy is this, for the effects of their new deity can be seen manifesting around them – the Ynnari can draw upon the souls within the spirit stones they wear to bolster their own abilities, siphon the power of those slain nearby to invigorate their attacks, and turn their foes to ashes and dust with the strange weapons and psychic powers they wield. They have learned the secrets of the dead, bringing them closer to their ancestors and the lost glories of their fallen race.

However, many see the Ynnari as corrupted by the very daemonic forces they seek to thwart, whilst others believe they are already dead inside. And perhaps they are right. Though the Ynnari seek to reforge Aeldari society in Ynnead's name and restore the glory of the ancient Aeldari race, their arrogant coercion of the metaphysical powers of their kind has alienated as many as it has united. Worse still, the danger they pose to the Dark Gods has seen the forces of Chaos – and especially those of Slaanesh – rise up like a tsunami of devilry in their hunger to consume them. Conflict and destruction erupts in the Ynnari's wake. Wherever they go, one thing stands out as a stark truth above all. As well as bringing hope, the Ynnari bring death – and in great measure.

YNNARI ARMY LIST

This section contains all of the datasheets that you will need in order to fight battles with your Ynnari miniatures. Each datasheet includes the characteristics profiles of the unit it describes, as well as any wargear and abilities it may have. The Strength from Death ability is common to all Ynnari units – it is described below and referenced on the datasheets.

ARMY OF THE REBORN

With the exception of <Haemonculus Coven> units, Urien Rakarth, Drazhar, Mandrakes and the Avatar of Khaine, any **Aeldari** unit can be part of an Ynnari army. Any unit that does so gains the **Ynnari** keyword. These cannot use any of the following abilities, and are not considered to have them: Ancient Doom, Battle Focus, Rising Crescendo, Power from Pain. Instead, **Infantry** and **Biker** units included in an Ynnari army gain the Strength from Death ability, as described below.

ABILITIES

Strength from Death

This ability is common to all **Ynnari Infantry** and **Ynnari Biker** units and the Yncarne. Each time a unit is completely destroyed within 7" of one or more units with this ability, except in the Morale phase, pick one of those units to make a Soulburst action. That unit can immediately do one of the following, even if it has already done so in this turn:

- The unit can move as if it were your Movement phase. It can Advance or Fall Back as part of this move.

- The unit can, if it is a **Psyker**, immediately attempt to manifest a single psychic power as if it were the Psychic phase.

- The unit can shoot as if it were your Shooting phase, even if it Advanced or Fell Back this turn.

- The unit can charge as if it were the Charge phase, even if it Advanced or Fell Back this turn (enemy units can fire Overwatch as normal). A unit cannot do this if it is within 1" of an enemy unit.

- The unit can fight as if it were the Fight phase.

Note that this means that a unit may be able to shoot or fight twice in the same turn.

A unit can only make a Soulburst action once per turn.

Ynnead's Will

Units with this ability can embark onto any **Aeldari Transport**, even though the transport in question might normally only permit models with other Faction keywords to do so. All other restrictions apply normally.

REVENANT DISCIPLINE

Before the battle, generate the psychic powers for **Psykers** that can use powers from the Revenant discipline using the table below. You can either roll a D3 to generate their powers randomly (re-roll any duplicate results), or you can select the psychic powers you wish the psyker to have.

REVENANT DISCIPLINE	
D3	**PSYCHIC POWER**
1	**Gaze of Ynnead** *Gaze of Ynnead* has a warp charge value of 8. If manifested, select a visible enemy unit within 18" of the psyker and roll a D6. On a 1, that unit suffers a mortal wound. On a 2-5 that unit suffers D3 mortal wounds. On a 6, that unit suffers D6 mortal wounds.
2	**Ancestors' Grace** *Ancestors' Grace* has a warp charge value of 5. If manifested, select a friendly **Ynnari** unit within 18" of the psyker. Until the start of your next Psychic phase, you can re-roll hit rolls of 1 for that unit.
3	**Word of the Phoenix** *Word of the Phoenix* has a warp charge value of 6. If manifested, select a friendly **Ynnari** unit within 18" of the psyker that has not made a Soulburst action this turn. That unit can immediately make a Soulburst action (see Strength from Death).

YVRAINE

NAME	M	WS	BS	S	T	W	A	Ld	Sv
Yvraine	8"	2+	2+	3	3	5	4	9	6+

Yvraine is a single model armed with Kha-vir, the Sword of Sorrows. Only one of this model may be included in your army.

WEAPON	RANGE	TYPE	S	AP	D	ABILITIES
Kha-vir, the Sword of Sorrows	Melee	Melee	+1	-2	D3	-

ABILITIES	Strength from Death, Ynnead's Will (pg 76)	**Herald of Ynnead:** Each time another **AELDARI** model is slain within 7" of Yvraine, roll a D6. On a 4+, Yvraine immediately regains a lost wound. If the model was a **PSYKER**, you can immediately generate another psychic power for Yvraine from the Revenant discipline.
	Runesuit: Yvraine has a 4+ invulnerable save.	
	Gyrinx Familiar: You can add 1 to all of Yvraine's Psychic tests and Deny the Witch tests.	

PSYKER	Yvraine can attempt to manifest two psychic powers in each friendly Psychic phase, and attempt to deny one psychic power in each enemy Psychic phase. She knows the *Smite* power and two psychic powers from the Revenant discipline (pg 76).

FACTION KEYWORDS	**AELDARI, YNNARI**
KEYWORDS	**CHARACTER, INFANTRY, PSYKER, YVRAINE**

THE VISARCH

NAME	M	WS	BS	S	T	W	A	Ld	Sv
The Visarch	8"	2+	2+	3	3	5	5	9	3+

The Visarch is a single model armed with Asu-var, the Sword of Silent Screams. Only one of this model may be included in your army.

WEAPON	RANGE	TYPE	S	AP	D	ABILITIES
Asu-var, the Sword of Silent Screams	Melee	Melee	+2	-3	D3	Enemy units that suffer any unsaved wounds from this weapon subtract 1 from their Leadership until the end of the turn.

ABILITIES	Strength from Death, Ynnead's Will (pg 76)	**Warden of Yvraine:** If Yvraine suffers a wound or mortal wound while the Visarch is within 3", you can choose for the Visarch to shield Yvraine. If you do, roll a D6. On a 2+ Yvraine does not suffer the wound, but the Visarch suffers a mortal wound.
	Champion of Ynnead: Each time another **AELDARI** model is slain within 7" of the Visarch, roll a D6. On a 4+, the Visarch immediately regains a lost wound. If that model was a **CHARACTER**, add 1 to the Visarch's Attacks characteristic for the rest of the battle (to a maximum Attacks characteristic of 7).	

FACTION KEYWORDS	**AELDARI, YNNARI**
KEYWORDS	**CHARACTER, INFANTRY, THE VISARCH**

THE YNCARNE

NAME	M	WS	BS	S	T	W	A	Ld	Sv
The Yncarne	8"	2+	2+	6	6	9	6	9	3+

The Yncarne is a single model armed with Vilith-zhar, the Sword of Souls. Only one of this model may be included in your army.

WEAPON	RANGE	TYPE	S	AP	D	ABILITIES
Vilith-zhar, the Sword of Souls	Melee	Melee	User	-4	D6	You can re-roll failed wound rolls for this weapon.

ABILITIES		
	Strength from Death (pg 76)	**Ynnead Stirs:** Friendly **Ynnari** units within 6" of the Yncarne automatically pass Morale tests. In addition, whenever a friendly **Ynnari** unit within 6" of the Yncarne suffers an unsaved wound or mortal wound, roll a D6. On a 6 that wound is ignored.
	Daemonic Avatar: The Yncarne has a 4+ invulnerable save.	
	Inevitable Death: When you set up the Yncarne, it must be set up in waiting rather than on the battlefield. When a unit (friend or foe) is completely destroyed, you may immediately set up the Yncarne as close as possible to the position of that unit, more than 1" from all enemy models. Each time a unit (friend or foe) is completely destroyed, you may immediately remove the Yncarne from the battlefield and set it up again as close as possible to the position of that unit, more than 1" from all enemy models. The Yncarne may not charge in the turn it is set up in this manner.	**Avatar of Ynnead:** Each time another **Aeldari** model is slain within 7" of the Yncarne, roll a D6. On a 4+, the Yncarne regains a wound lost earlier in the battle.

PSYKER	The Yncarne can attempt to manifest two psychic powers in each friendly Psychic phase, and attempt to deny one psychic power in each enemy Psychic phase. It knows the *Smite* power and two psychic powers from the Revenant discipline (pg 76).
FACTION KEYWORDS	**Aeldari, Ynnari**
KEYWORDS	**Character, Monster, Daemon, Fly, Psyker, The Yncarne**

The Ynnari see themselves as the last hope of the Aeldari, and they will destroy any who threaten the resurgence of their ancient race.

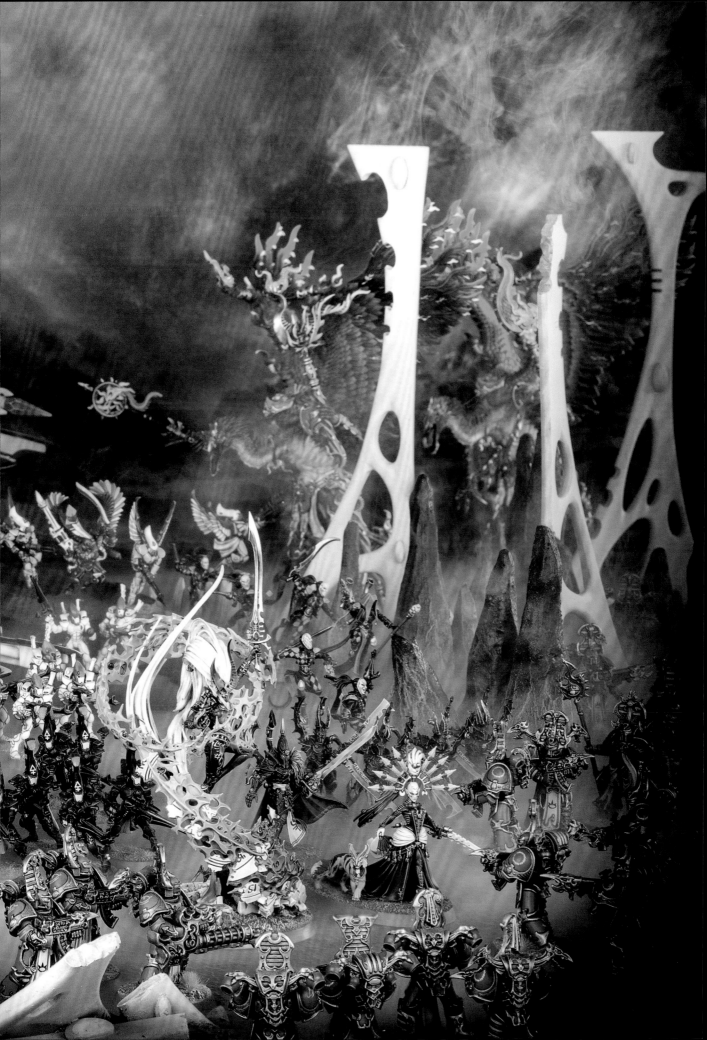

NECRONS

Advancing in inexorable lockstep come the deathless legions of the Necrons. Eldritch energy weapons crackle and howl, erasing swathes of the enemy. Godlike beings twist reality to their will. The living fall to dust, swept away by ancient powers beyond comprehension. The Necrons have risen to reclaim the stars, and none shall stand in their way.

Ancient beyond mortal comprehension, the Necrons emerge from the shadows of galactic prehistory to reclaim their empire. They wield superweapons with the power to channel the might of stars, align planets at will or pervert the laws of reality itself. Their legions of mindlessly loyal warriors slaughter their enemies without mercy. Arrogant and cruel, the immortal nobility of the Necrons view the galaxy's sentient races as little but parasites, impudent vermin to be swept aside by their triumphal return. Though scattered and time-worn from millennia of self-imposed hibernation, more Necrons rise from their slumbers with every passing year, and their dynasties grow mighty once more. In centuries long forgotten, every living thing knew to fear the wrath of the all-powerful Necrons. In this dark new era, they are learning to do so again.

THE WAR IN HEAVEN

Millions of years before Mankind's ancestors had even crawled from the primordial ooze, the empire of the Necrontyr spanned the stars. Short-lived thanks to the radiation of their home world's star, belligerent and arrogant in their martial might, the Necrontyr began a war with the Old Ones for their secrets of eternal life. It soon proved to be a war that they could not win. In his desperation, the Necrontyr leader – Szarekh, the Silent King – turned to the C'tan for aid. These ancient star gods offered a devil's bargain – through biotransference, the C'tan would take the Necrontyr race and rehouse their minds within enduring bodies of living metal that would last for aeons. In return, the Necrontyr would help the C'tan to destroy the Old Ones once and for all. Szarekh agreed, and so damned himself and his people for all eternity.

The C'tan made good upon their promise, and the Necrontyr were transformed into the Necrons. Yet though their minds made the transition to their new bodies, the souls of the Necrontyr burned away along with their flesh. Only the most highly placed of the Silent King's people retained the full range of sentience, emotion and reason, with the lower classes reduced to little more than obedient automata. Worse, all found themselves shackled to the will of the C'tan.

The Necrontyr got their wish, however. The war in heaven turned against the Old Ones, who were forced into exile by the resurgent Necrons and their C'tan allies. It is not recorded how Szarekh succeeded in rebelling at the last, but rebel he did. Desperate to earn redemption for the horrors he had wrought upon his people, the Silent King unleashed the full might of his race's star-killing weaponry to shatter the C'tan into myriad divine shards. These the Necrons bound to their will, or else trapped within tesseract labyrinths for all eternity, a fitting punishment for those who had sought to entrap the Necrontyr forever.

The War in Heaven decimated the Necron legions. With fresh foes closing on every side, the Aeldari chief amongst them, they elected to retreat into immense stasis-crypts, hidden far beneath the surfaces of their many worlds. They would slumber through the millennia, waiting until the empires of their enemies had been brought to their knees by the slow turning of time. Only then would the Necrons emerge once more, into a galaxy ripe for final conquest.

Matters, as it transpired, turned out somewhat differently...

AWAKENING

Thousands of years have passed since the first Necrons rose from their slumbers to find themselves in a galaxy not scoured of life, but teeming with it. The effects of the churning warp, the toll taken by the Age of Strife and millennia of galactic war, and the sheer grinding passage of time had destroyed some stasis-crypts entirely. Those that endured were surrounded by the warring empires of the younger races, who in many cases had profaned the tomb worlds themselves with their presence.

The soulless warriors of the Necron dynasties arose, emerging from beneath the cities and fortresses of the terrified younger races and exterminating them without mercy. Immense tomb ships smashed their way up through continental plates, or rose from the depths of fathomless ocean trenches to bear the Necrons out into the galaxy once more.

Deranged or disoriented by their timeless sleep, the nobility of each Necron dynasty have set about the reconquest of their ancient empires in whatever fashion seems best to them. Some seek to recapture the worlds that were once theirs, others to rebuild their star-killing superweapons, to purge the lesser races, or to awaken further tomb complexes. Much has been lost, but the Necrons remain convinced of their supremacy, and their right to rule.

Of the Silent King there has been no recorded sign. Without his unifying influence the scattered Necron dynasties war with each other as often as they find common cause. Yet great leaders have emerged from amongst the ranks of each dynasty's nobility, figures such as Imotekh the Stormlord and Nemesor Zahndrekh driving the lesser races before them with tireless martial efficiency. The Necrons mean to make the galaxy theirs once again, and they are not of a mind to share their domain with the lesser races who would despoil the timeless perfection of Necron dominance.

REANIMATION PROTOCOLS

The Necrons are not creatures of flesh and blood, but soulless warriors whose immortal forms are forged from living metal. As such, they are almost impervious to destruction, and their bodies are swift to heal even the gravest of wounds. Given time, severed limbs reattach, armour plating reknits and shattered mechanical organs are rebuilt. The only way to assure a Necron's destruction is to overwhelm its ability to self-repair, to inflict such massive damage that its systems cannot keep pace. Even should irreplaceable damage occur, the Necron will often simply 'phase out' – automated teleport beams return it to the safety of the stasis-crypts, where it remains in storage until such time as repairs can be carried out by waiting Canoptek constructs.

The sciences by which such feats are achieved remain a mystery to outsiders, for the Necrons do not share their secrets with lesser races and have set contingencies to prevent their supreme technologies from falling into the wrong hands. Should a fallen warrior fail to phase out, it self-destructs and is consumed by a blaze of emerald light. Outwardly, this appears little different to the glow of teleportation, leaving the enemy to wonder whether the Necron has finally been destroyed, or merely retreated to its tomb.

THE SAUTEKH DYNASTY

Imotekh the Stormlord rules the Sautekh Dynasty with an iron fist and a cold, analytical mind. The greatest strategist the galaxy has ever known, Imotekh leads campaigns of conquest in which entire star systems are but playing pieces. Always the Stormlord remains three steps ahead of his enemies, herding the younger races like cattle to the slaughter with contemptuous ease.

The Sautekh Dynasty is arguably the greatest remaining Necron dynasty – huge, powerful, and belligerently wakeful. Imotekh has made full use of these advantages, spreading his dynastic dominion across the stars at a fearsome pace. In this advance Imotekh has slain scores of so-called heroes and saviours in personal combat. If Imotekh could be said to possess a weakness it is his desire to humble his foes by his own hand, and it may yet prove his undoing. But then, as Imotekh himself asserts, when one can simply be reborn from the stasis crypts time and time again, what need has one to fear death in the service of ultimate victory?

NECRONS ARMY LIST

This section contains all of the datasheets that you will need in order to fight battles with your Necron miniatures. Each datasheet includes the characteristics profiles of the unit it describes, as well as any wargear and special abilities it may have. Some abilities are common to several Necron units, in which case they are described below and referenced on the datasheets themselves.

KEYWORDS

Throughout this section you will come across a keyword that is within angular brackets, specifically <Dynasty>. This is shorthand for a keyword of your own choosing, as described below.

<Dynasty>

Most Necrons belong to a dynasty. Some datasheets specify what dynasty a Necron unit is drawn from (e.g. Imotekh the Stormlord is from the Sautekh Dynasty, and so has the Sautekh keyword). If a Necron datasheet has the <Dynasty> keyword, you must nominate which dynasty that unit is from. There are many different dynasties to choose from; you can use any of the dynasties described in our books, or make up your own if you prefer. You then simply replace the <Dynasty> keyword in every instance on that unit's datasheet with the name of your chosen dynasty.

For example, if you were to include a Lord in your army, and you decided it was from the Nihilakh dynasty, then its <Dynasty> keyword is changed to Nihilakh, and its 'The Lord's Will' ability would say 'You can re-roll failed Morale tests for friendly Nihilakh units within 6" of this model.'

ABILITIES

The following abilities are common to several Necron units:

Reanimation Protocols

Roll a D6 for each slain model from this unit (unless the whole unit has been completely destroyed) at the beginning of your turn. On a 5+, the model's reanimation protocols activate and it is returned to this unit, otherwise they remain inactive (although you can roll again at the start of each of your subsequent turns). When a model's reanimation protocols activate, set it up model in unit coherency with any model from this unit that has not returned to the unit as a result of reanimation protocols this turn, and more than 1" from enemy models. If you cannot do this because there is no room to place the model, do not set it up.

Living Metal

At the beginning of your turn, this unit recovers 1 wound lost earlier in the battle.

POWERS OF THE C'TAN

Before the battle begins, generate the Powers of the C'tan for each **C'tan Shard** using the table below. You can either roll a D3 to generate their powers randomly (re-roll any duplicate results), or you can select the powers you wish the C'tan Shard to have.

POWERS OF THE C'TAN

D3	POWER OF THE C'TAN
1	**Antimatter Meteor** Roll a D6; on a 2+ the closest visible enemy unit within 24" of the C'tan Shard suffers D3 mortal wounds.
2	**Time's Arrow** Pick a visible enemy unit within 24" of the C'tan Shard and roll a D6. If the result is higher than that unit's Wounds characteristic, one model from that unit is slain.
3	**Seismic Assault** Roll a D6 for each model in the closest enemy unit within 24" of the C'tan Shard. For each roll of 6 that unit suffers a mortal wound.

WARGEAR

Some of the Necron units you will find on the following pages reference the following wargear list. When this is the case, the unit may take any item from the list below. The profiles for the weapons in this list can be found in the appendix (pg 128).

MELEE WEAPONS

- Hyperphase sword
- Voidblade
- Warscythe

IMOTEKH THE STORMLORD

12 POWER

NAME	M	WS	BS	S	T	W	A	Ld	Sv
Imotekh the Stormlord	5"	2+	2+	5	5	6	3	9	2+

Imotekh the Stormlord is a single model armed with the Staff of the Destroyer and a gauntlet of fire. Only one of this model may be included in your army.

WEAPON	RANGE	TYPE	S	AP	D	ABILITIES
Gauntlet of fire	8"	Assault D6	4	0	1	This weapon automatically hits its target.
Staff of the Destroyer (shooting)	18"	Assault 3	6	-3	2	-
Staff of the Destroyer (melee)	Melee	Melee	User	-3	2	-

ABILITIES		
	Living Metal (pg 84)	**Phase Shifter:** Imotekh the Stormlord has a 4+ invulnerable save.
	Bloodswarm Necroscarabs: You can re-roll hit rolls of 1 for friendly units of **SAUTEKH** Flayed Ones that are within 12" of Imotekh the Stormlord.	**Lord of the Storm:** Once per battle in your Shooting phase, Imotekh can call the storm: when he does so pick an enemy unit within 48" of Imotekh, other than a **CHARACTER**, and roll a D6. On a 1 nothing happens, but on a 2+ that unit suffers that many mortal wounds. Then roll a D6 for each enemy unit within 6" of that unit. On a roll of 6, that unit suffers D3 mortal wounds.
	My Will Be Done: At the beginning of each of your turns, choose a friendly **NECRON INFANTRY** unit within 6" of Imotekh the Stormlord. You can add 1 to the Advance, charge and hit rolls of that unit until the beginning of your next turn. A unit can only be affected by this ability once in each turn.	**Undying:** Imotekh the Stormlord regains D3 lost wounds at the beginning of your turn, rather than 1, from his Living Metal ability.

FACTION KEYWORDS	**NECRONS, SAUTEKH**
KEYWORDS	**CHARACTER, INFANTRY, OVERLORD, IMOTEKH THE STORMLORD**

Imotekh, the phaeron of the Sautekh Dynasty, is a military genius whose campaigns of terror have conquered countless star systems.

OVERLORD

7 POWER

NAME	M	WS	BS	S	T	W	A	Ld	Sv
Overlord	5"	2+	2+	5	5	5	3	10	3+

An Overlord is a single model armed with a staff of light.

WEAPON	RANGE	TYPE	S	AP	D	ABILITIES
Staff of light (shooting)	12"	Assault 3	5	-2	1	-
Staff of light (melee)	Melee	Melee	User	-2	1	-

WARGEAR OPTIONS	• This model may replace its staff of light with an item from the *Melee Weapons* list.
	• This model may take a resurrection orb.

ABILITIES	Living Metal (pg 84)	Phase Shifter: This model has a 4+ invulnerable save.
	Resurrection Orb: If this model has a resurrection orb, once per battle, immediately after you have made your Reanimation Protocols rolls, you can make Reanimation Protocol rolls for models from a friendly <DYNASTY> INFANTRY unit within 3" of this model.	**My Will Be Done:** At the beginning of each of your turns, choose a friendly <DYNASTY> INFANTRY unit within 6" of this model. You can add 1 to the Advance, charge and hit rolls of that unit until the beginning of your next turn. A unit can only be affected by this ability once in each turn.

FACTION KEYWORDS	NECRONS, <DYNASTY>
KEYWORDS	CHARACTER, INFANTRY, OVERLORD

LORD

5 POWER

NAME	M	WS	BS	S	T	W	A	Ld	Sv
Lord	5"	3+	3+	5	5	4	3	10	3+

A Lord is a single model armed with a staff of light.

WEAPON	RANGE	TYPE	S	AP	D	ABILITIES
Staff of light (shooting)	12"	Assault 3	5	-2	1	-
Staff of light (melee)	Melee	Melee	User	-2	1	-

WARGEAR OPTIONS	• This model may replace its staff of light with an item from the *Melee Weapons* list.
	• This model may take a resurrection orb.

ABILITIES	Living Metal (pg 84)	**Resurrection Orb:** If this model has a resurrection orb, once per battle, immediately after you have made your Reanimation Protocols rolls, you can make Reanimation Protocol rolls for models from a friendly <DYNASTY> INFANTRY unit within 3" of this model.
	The Lord's Will: You can re-roll failed Morale tests for friendly <DYNASTY> units within 6" of this model.	

FACTION KEYWORDS	NECRONS, <DYNASTY>
KEYWORDS	CHARACTER, INFANTRY, LORD

CRYPTEK

6 POWER

NAME	M	WS	BS	S	T	W	A	Ld	Sv
Cryptek	5"	3+	3+	4	4	4	1	10	4+

A Cryptek is a single model armed with a staff of light.

WEAPON	RANGE	TYPE	S	AP	D	ABILITIES
Staff of light (shooting)	12"	Assault 3	5	-2	1	-
Staff of light (melee)	Melee	Melee	User	-2	1	-

ABILITIES	**Living Metal** (pg 84)	**Technomancer:** Add 1 to all Reanimation Protocol rolls for models from friendly <Dynasty> units within 3" of any friendly <Dynasty> Crypteks.
	Chronometron: Friendly <Dynasty> Infantry units within 3" of this unit have a 5+ invulnerable save against ranged weapons.	

FACTION KEYWORDS	Necrons, <Dynasty>
KEYWORDS	Character, Infantry, Cryptek

DESTROYER LORD

8 POWER

NAME	M	WS	BS	S	T	W	A	Ld	Sv
Destroyer Lord	10"	3+	3+	5	6	6	4	10	3+

A Destroyer Lord is a single model armed with a staff of light.

WEAPON	RANGE	TYPE	S	AP	D	ABILITIES
Staff of light (shooting)	12"	Assault 3	5	-2	1	-
Staff of light (melee)	Melee	Melee	User	-2	1	-

WARGEAR OPTIONS	• This model may replace its staff of light with an item from the *Melee Weapons* list. • This model may take either a phylactery or a resurrection orb.

ABILITIES	**Living Metal** (pg 84)	**Phylactery:** A model with a phylactery regains D3 lost wounds at the beginning of your turn, rather than 1, from their Living Metal ability.
	Hardwired Hatred: You can re-roll hit rolls of 1 for this model.	
	United in Hatred: You can re-roll wound rolls of 1 in the Shooting phase for this model and models from friendly <Dynasty> Destroyer and <Dynasty> Heavy Destroyer units within 6".	**Resurrection Orb:** If this model has a resurrection orb, once per battle, immediately after you have made your Reanimation Protocols rolls, you can make Reanimation Protocol rolls for models from a friendly <Dynasty> Infantry unit within 3" of this model.
	Phase Shifter: This model has a 4+ invulnerable save.	

FACTION KEYWORDS	Necrons, <Dynasty>
KEYWORDS	Character, Infantry, Fly, Destroyer Lord

NEMESOR ZAHNDREKH

9 POWER

NAME	M	WS	BS	S	T	W	A	Ld	Sv
Nemesor Zahndrekh	5"	2+	2+	5	5	6	3	10	2+

Nemesor Zahndrekh is a single model armed with a staff of light. Only one of this model may be included in your army.

WEAPON	RANGE	TYPE	S	AP	D	ABILITIES
Staff of light (shooting)	12"	Assault 3	5	-2	1	-
Staff of light (melee)	Melee	Melee	User	-2	1	-

ABILITIES

Living Metal (pg 84)

Counter Tactics: At the beginning of your opponent's turn, choose one enemy **CHARACTER** within 12" of Nemesor Zahndrekh. Any aura abilities that character has cannot be used until the beginning of your opponent's next turn.

Phase Shifter: Nemesor Zahndrekh has a 4+ invulnerable save.

My Will Be Done: At the beginning of each of your turns, choose a friendly **SAUTEKH INFANTRY** unit within 6" of Nemesor Zahndrekh. You can add 1 to the Advance, charge and hit rolls of that unit until the beginning of your next turn. A unit can only be affected by this ability once in each turn.

Transient Madness: Roll a D3 for Nemesor Zahndrekh at the beginning of each of your turns and consult the following table. Choose a friendly **SAUTEKH INFANTRY** unit within 6" of Nemesor Zahndrekh to benefit from the relevant ability until the beginning of your next turn.

D3	Result
1	**Avenge the Fallen:** Models with this ability have +1 Attack.
2	**Quell the Rebellion:** Models with this ability improve their Ballistic Skill by 1 (e.g. a Ballistic Skill of 3+ becomes 2+, etc.).
3	**Solarmills? Charge!:** You can re-roll failed charge rolls for a unit with this ability.

FACTION KEYWORDS	NECRONS, SAUTEKH
KEYWORDS	CHARACTER, INFANTRY, OVERLORD, NEMESOR ZAHNDREKH

VARGARD OBYRON

8 POWER

NAME	M	WS	BS	S	T	W	A	Ld	Sv
Vargard Obyron	5"	2+	3+	5	5	6	3	10	2+

Vargard Obyron is a single model armed with a warscythe. Only one of this model may be included in your army.

WEAPON	RANGE	TYPE	S	AP	D	ABILITIES
Warscythe	Melee	Melee	+2	-4	2	-

ABILITIES

Living Metal (pg 84)

Cleaving Counterblow: If Vargard Obyron is slain during the Fight phase, do not remove his model until the end of the phase. He can still fight in this phase, if he has not already done so.

The Lord's Will: You can re-roll failed Morale tests for friendly **SAUTEKH** units within 6" of Vargard Obyron.

Ghostwalk Mantle: At the end of any of your Movement phases, you can remove Vargard Obyron and a friendly **SAUTEKH INFANTRY** unit within 6" of Vargard Obyron from the battlefield and set them up so that all models are within 6" of Nemesor Zahndrekh and more than 1" from the enemy.

The Vargard's Duty: Roll a D6 each time Nemesor Zahndrekh loses a wound whilst he is within 3" of Vargard Obyron; on a 2+ Obyron can intercept that hit – Zahndrekh does not lose a wound but Obyron suffers a mortal wound.

FACTION KEYWORDS	NECRONS, SAUTEKH
KEYWORDS	CHARACTER, INFANTRY, LORD, VARGARD OBYRON

ILLUMINOR SZERAS

NAME	M	WS	BS	S	T	W	A	Ld	Sv
Illuminor Szeras	6"	3+	3+	4	4	5	4	10	3+

Illuminor Szeras is a single model armed with the Eldritch Lance. Only one of this model may be included in your army.

WEAPON	RANGE	TYPE	S	AP	D	ABILITIES
Eldritch Lance (shooting)	36"	Assault 1	8	-4	D6	-
Eldritch Lance (melee)	Melee	Melee	User	-2	1	-

ABILITIES	
	Living Metal (pg 84)

Master Technomancer: Add 1 to all Reanimation Protocol rolls for models from friendly **NECRON** units within 3" of Illuminor Szeras. A unit cannot benefit from both the Master Technomancer and Technomancer abilities in the same turn.

Mechanical Augmentation: At the end of each of his Movement phases, Illuminor Szeras can augment one unit of **NECRON** Warriors or Immortals that is within 1" of him. Roll a D3 to see what augmentation the unit gains for the rest of the battle:

D3	Augmentation
1	+1 Strength
2	+1 Toughness
3	Ballistic Skill improved by 1 (e.g. a Ballistic Skill of 3+ becomes 2+, etc.)

A unit can only be enhanced by Mechanical Augmentation once per battle.

FACTION KEYWORDS	NECRONS
KEYWORDS	CHARACTER, INFANTRY, CRYPTEK, ILLUMINOR SZERAS

ORIKAN THE DIVINER

8 POWER

NAME	M	WS	BS	S	T	W	A	Ld	Sv
Orikan the Diviner	5"	3+	3+	4	4	5	2	10	4+
Orikan Empowered	5"	2+	2+	7	7	7	4	10	4+

Orikan the Diviner is a single model armed with the Staff of Tomorrow. Only one of this model may be included in your army.

WEAPON	RANGE	TYPE	S	AP	D	ABILITIES
Staff of Tomorrow	Melee	Melee	User	-3	D3	You can re-roll failed hit rolls for this weapon.

ABILITIES		
	Living Metal (pg 84)	**The Stars Are Right:** Roll a D6 at the start of each of your turns. If the result is less than the current battle round number, Orikan uses the Orikan Empowered profile for the rest of the game (though any damage he has sustained is carried over).
	Master Chronomancer: Friendly **SAUTEKH INFANTRY** units within 6" of Orikan the Diviner have a 5+ invulnerable save.	
	Technomancer: Add 1 to all Reanimation Protocol rolls for models from friendly **SAUTEKH** units within 3" of any friendly **SAUTEKH CRYPTEKS**.	

FACTION KEYWORDS	**NECRONS, SAUTEKH**
KEYWORDS	**CHARACTER, INFANTRY, CRYPTEK, ORIKAN THE DIVINER**

Orikan the Diviner is a powerful astromancer, able to glimpse the future and even travel into the past to alter events.

ANRAKYR THE TRAVELLER

9 POWER

NAME	M	WS	BS	S	T	W	A	Ld	Sv
Anrakyr the Traveller	5"	2+	2+	6	5	6	3	10	3+

Anrakyr the Traveller is a single model armed with a tachyon arrow and a warscythe. Only one of this model may be included in your army.

WEAPON	RANGE	TYPE	S	AP	D	ABILITIES
Tachyon arrow	120"	Assault 1	10	-5	D6	This weapon can only be used once per battle.
Warscythe	Melee	Melee	+2	-4	2	-

ABILITIES	Living Metal (pg 84)	Phase Shifter: Anrakyr the Traveller has a 4+ invulnerable save.
	Lord of the Pyrrhian Legions: Add 1 to the Attacks characteristic of friendly **NECRON INFANTRY** units within 3" of Anrakyr the Traveller.	**My Will Be Done:** At the beginning of each of your turns, choose a friendly **NECRON INFANTRY** unit within 6" of Anrakyr the Traveller. You can add 1 to the Advance, charge and hit rolls of that unit until the beginning of your next turn. A unit can only be affected by this ability once in each turn.
	Mind in the Machine: At the start of your Shooting phase, choose an enemy **VEHICLE** within 12" of Anrakyr the Traveller and roll a D6. On a 4+, choose one of that vehicle's weapons. You may shoot with that weapon at another enemy unit. The weapon fires using the vehicle's Ballistic Skill.	

FACTION KEYWORDS	NECRONS
KEYWORDS	**CHARACTER, INFANTRY, OVERLORD, ANRAKYR THE TRAVELLER**

TRAZYN THE INFINITE

7 POWER

NAME	M	WS	BS	S	T	W	A	Ld	Sv
Trazyn the Infinite	5"	2+	2+	5	5	6	3	10	3+

Trazyn the Infinite is a single model armed with the Empathic Obliterator. Only one of this model may be included in your army.

WEAPON	RANGE	TYPE	S	AP	D	ABILITIES
Empathic Obliterator	Melee	Melee	+2	-1	D3	If a **CHARACTER** is slain by an attack from this weapon, each unit within 6" (friend or foe) that is from the same Faction as the slain character suffers D3 mortal wounds.

ABILITIES	Living Metal (pg 84)	**Surrogate Hosts:** If Trazyn the Infinite is slain, roll a D6. On a 2+, you may choose another friendly **NECRON INFANTRY CHARACTER** (other than **CHARACTERS** that you can only include once in your army). Remove that model as if it were slain and place Trazyn in its place with D3 wounds remaining. If no such **CHARACTERS** remain, or you rolled a 1, remove Trazyn the Infinite as a casualty as normal.
	Phase Shifter: Trazyn the Infinite has a 4+ invulnerable save.	
	My Will Be Done: At the beginning of each of your turns, choose a friendly **NIHILAKH INFANTRY** unit within 6" of Trazyn the Infinite. You can add 1 to the Advance, charge and hit rolls of that unit until the beginning of your next turn. A unit can only be affected by this ability once in each turn.	

FACTION KEYWORDS	NECRONS, NIHILAKH
KEYWORDS	**CHARACTER, INFANTRY, OVERLORD, TRAZYN THE INFINITE**

CATACOMB COMMAND BARGE

NAME	M	WS	BS	S	T	W	A	Ld	Sv
Catacomb Command Barge	12"	2+	2+	5	6	8	3	10	3+

This unit contains 1 Catacomb Command Barge, commanded by an Overlord.
- The Overlord is armed with a staff of light.
- The Catacomb Command Barge is equipped with a gauss cannon.

WEAPON	RANGE	TYPE	S	AP	D	ABILITIES
Gauss cannon	24"	Heavy 2	5	-3	D3	-
Staff of light (shooting)	12"	Assault 3	5	-2	1	-
Tesla cannon	24"	Assault 3	6	0	1	Each hit roll of 6+ with this weapon causes 3 hits instead of 1.
Staff of light (melee)	Melee	Melee	User	-2	1	-

WARGEAR OPTIONS	
	• The Overlord may replace their staff of light with an item from the *Melee Weapons* list.
	• The Overlord may take a resurrection orb.
	• The Catacomb Command Barge may replace its gauss cannon with a tesla cannon.

ABILITIES	
	Living Metal (pg 84)
	Wave of Command: At the beginning of each of your turns, choose a friendly <Dynasty> Infantry unit within 12" of this model. You can add 1 to the Advance, charge and hit rolls of that unit until the beginning of your next turn. A unit cannot be affected by Wave of Command and My Will Be Done in the same turn.
	Quantum Shielding: Each time this model suffers damage from an unsaved wound, roll a D6. If the result is less than the damage inflicted by the attack, the damage is ignored (e.g. if this model suffers 4 damage, if you then roll a 3 or less the damage is ignored).
	Resurrection Orb: If this model has a resurrection orb, once per battle, immediately after you have made your Reanimation Protocols rolls, you can make Reanimation Protocol rolls for models from a friendly <Dynasty> Infantry unit within 3" of this model.
	Explodes: If this model is reduced to 0 wounds, roll a D6 before removing it from the battlefield. On a 6 it explodes, and each unit within 3" suffers a mortal wound.

FACTION KEYWORDS	Necrons, <Dynasty>
KEYWORDS	Vehicle, Overlord, Fly, Catacomb Command Barge

A Catacomb Command Barge bears a Necron Overlord into battle – an imposing throne from which he can direct his forces.

NECRON WARRIORS

6 POWER

NAME	M	WS	BS	S	T	W	A	Ld	Sv
Necron Warrior	5"	3+	3+	4	4	1	1	10	4+

This unit contains 10 Necron Warriors. It may include up to 10 additional Necron Warriors (**Power Rating +6**). Each model is equipped with a gauss flayer.

WEAPON	RANGE	TYPE	S	AP	D	ABILITIES
Gauss flayer	24"	Rapid Fire 1	4	-1	1	-

ABILITIES	**Reanimation Protocols** (pg 84)
FACTION KEYWORDS	NECRONS, <DYNASTY>
KEYWORDS	INFANTRY, WARRIORS

IMMORTALS

4 POWER

NAME	M	WS	BS	S	T	W	A	Ld	Sv
Immortal	5"	3+	3+	4	4	1	1	10	3+

This unit contains 5 Immortals. It can include up to 5 additional Immortals (**Power Rating +4**). Each model is equipped with a gauss blaster.

WEAPON	RANGE	TYPE	S	AP	D	ABILITIES
Gauss blaster	24"	Rapid Fire 1	5	-2	1	-
Tesla carbine	24"	Assault 2	5	0	1	Each hit roll of 6+ with this weapon causes 3 hits instead of 1.

WARGEAR OPTIONS	• The entire unit may replace their gauss blasters with tesla carbines.
ABILITIES	**Reanimation Protocols** (pg 84)
FACTION KEYWORDS	NECRONS, <DYNASTY>
KEYWORDS	INFANTRY, IMMORTALS

LYCHGUARD

8 POWER

NAME	M	WS	BS	S	T	W	A	Ld	Sv
Lychguard	5"	3+	3+	5	5	2	2	10	3+

This unit contains 5 Lychguard. It can include up to 5 additional Lychguard (**Power Rating +8**). Each model is armed with a warscythe.

WEAPON	RANGE	TYPE	S	AP	D	ABILITIES
Hyperphase sword	Melee	Melee	User	-3	1	-
Warscythe	Melee	Melee	+2	-4	2	-

WARGEAR OPTIONS	• The entire unit may replace their warscythes with hyperphase swords and dispersion shields.
ABILITIES	**Reanimation Protocols** (pg 84) **Dispersion Shield:** A model equipped with a dispersion shield has a 4+ invulnerable save.	**Guardian Protocols:** Roll a D6 each time a friendly <DYNASTY> CHARACTER loses a wound whilst they are within 3" of this unit; on a 2+ a model from this unit can intercept that hit – the character does not lose a wound but this unit suffers a mortal wound.
FACTION KEYWORDS	NECRONS, <DYNASTY>
KEYWORDS	INFANTRY, LYCHGUARD

DEATHMARKS

5 POWER

NAME	M	WS	BS	S	T	W	A	Ld	Sv
Deathmarks	5"	3+	3+	4	4	1	1	10	3+

This unit contains 5 Deathmarks. It can include up to 5 additional Deathmarks (**Power Rating +5**). Each model is armed with a synaptic disintegrator.

WEAPON	RANGE	TYPE	S	AP	D	ABILITIES
Synaptic disintegrator	24"	Rapid Fire 1	4	0	1	This weapon may target a **CHARACTER** even if it is not the closest enemy unit. Each time you roll a wound roll of 6+ for this weapon, the target suffers a mortal wound in addition to any other damage.

ABILITIES	Reanimation Protocols (pg 84)	**Ethereal Interception:** When an enemy unit is set up (other than during deployment or when disembarking) you can immediately set up a unit of Deathmarks that was set up in a hyperspace oubliette on the battlefield, anywhere more than 9" away from any enemy models and within 12" of the enemy unit that has just been set up. You can then make a shooting attack with this unit as if it were your Shooting phase, but this attack must target the enemy unit that was just set up.
	Hunters from Hyperspace: During deployment, you can set up a unit of Deathmarks in a hyperspace oubliette instead of placing them on the battlefield. At the end of any of your Movement phases the Deathmarks can slip back into reality – set them up anywhere on the battlefield that is more than 9" away from any enemy models.

FACTION KEYWORDS	NECRONS, <DYNASTY>
KEYWORDS	INFANTRY, DEATHMARKS

FLAYED ONES

5 POWER

NAME	M	WS	BS	S	T	W	A	Ld	Sv
Flayed One	5"	3+	6+	4	4	1	4	10	4+

This unit contains 5 Flayed Ones. It can include up to 5 additional Flayed Ones (**Power Rating +5**), up to 10 additional Flayed Ones (**Power Rating +10**) or up to 15 additional Flayed Ones (**Power Rating +15**). Each model is armed with flayer claws.

WEAPON	RANGE	TYPE	S	AP	D	ABILITIES
Flayer claws	Melee	Melee	User	0	1	You can re-roll failed wound rolls for this weapon.

ABILITIES	Reanimation Protocols (pg 84)	**Haunting Horrors:** During deployment, you can set up a unit of Flayed Ones in a charnel pocket-dimension instead of placing it on the battlefield. At the end of any of your Movement phases the Flayed Ones can crawl out into reality – set them up anywhere on the battlefield that is more than 9" away from any enemy models.
	Flesh Hunger: When your opponent takes a Morale test for an enemy unit within 3" of any units of Flayed Ones, they must add 1 to the roll.

FACTION KEYWORDS	NECRONS, <DYNASTY>
KEYWORDS	INFANTRY, FLAYED ONES

Driven to savagery by an ancient madness, Flayed Ones delight in tearing the flesh from their prey with razor-sharp talons.

TRIARCH PRAETORIANS

8 POWER

NAME	M	WS	BS	S	T	W	A	Ld	Sv
Triarch Praetorian	10"	3+	3+	5	5	2	2	10	3+

This unit contains 5 Triarch Praetorians. It can include up to 5 additional Triarch Praetorians (**Power Rating +8**). Each model is armed with a rod of covenant.

WEAPON	RANGE	TYPE	S	AP	D	ABILITIES
Particle caster	12"	Pistol 1	6	0	1	-
Rod of covenant (shooting)	12"	Assault 1	5	-3	1	-
Rod of covenant (melee)	Melee	Melee	User	-3	1	-
Voidblade	Melee	Melee	User	-3	1	-

WARGEAR OPTIONS	• The entire unit may replace their rods of covenant with voidblades and particle casters.
ABILITIES	Reanimation Protocols (pg 84) **A Purpose Unshakeable:** This unit automatically passes Morale tests.
FACTION KEYWORDS	NECRONS
KEYWORDS	INFANTRY, FLY, TRIARCH PRAETORIANS

TRIARCH STALKER

8 POWER

DAMAGE
Some of this model's characteristics change as it suffers damage, as shown below:

REMAINING W	M	WS	BS
6-10+	10"	3+	3+
3-5	8"	4+	4+
1-2	6"	5+	5+

NAME	M	WS	BS	S	T	W	A	Ld	Sv
Triarch Stalker	*	*	*	7	6	10	3	10	3+

A Triarch Stalker is a single model equipped with a heat ray and massive forelimbs.

WEAPON	RANGE	TYPE	S	AP	D	ABILITIES
Heat ray	When attacking with this weapon, choose one of the profiles below.					
- Dispersed	8"	Heavy D6	5	-1	1	When you use this profile, this weapon automatically hits its target.
- Focused	24"	Heavy 2	8	-4	D6	When you use this profile, if the target is within half range, roll two dice when inflicting damage with it and discard the lowest result.
Particle shredder	24"	Heavy 6	7	-1	D3	-
Twin heavy gauss cannon	36"	Heavy 2	9	-4	D6	-
Massive forelimbs	Melee	Melee	User	-1	D3	-

WARGEAR OPTIONS	• This model may replace its heat ray with a particle shredder or a twin heavy gauss cannon.
ABILITIES	Living Metal (pg 84) **Quantum Shielding:** Each time this model suffers damage from an unsaved wound, roll a D6. If the result is less than the damage inflicted by the attack, the damage is ignored (e.g. if this model suffers 4 damage, if you then roll a 3 or less the damage is ignored).	**Targeting Relay:** You can re-roll hit rolls of 1 for any friendly NECRON unit that makes a shooting attack against a unit that has already been attacked by any Triarch Stalkers in this phase.
FACTION KEYWORDS	NECRONS
KEYWORDS	VEHICLE, TRIARCH STALKER

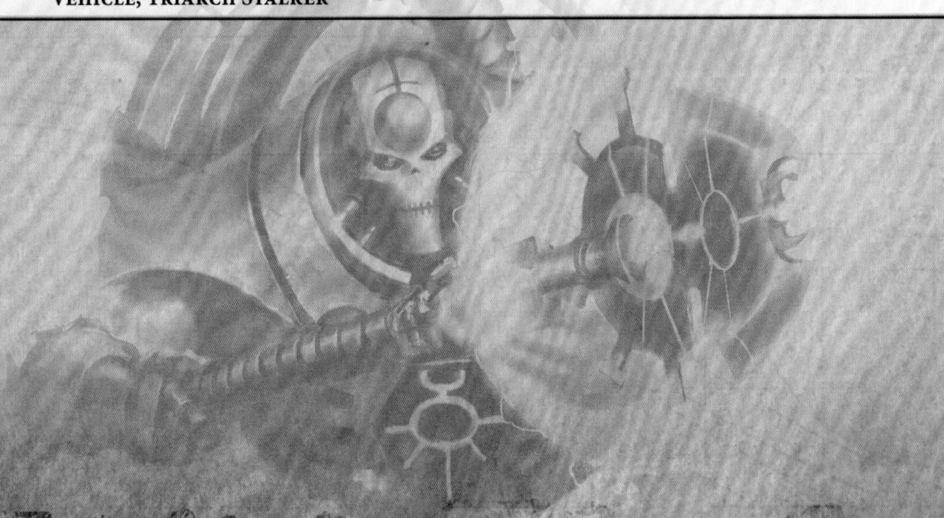

C'TAN SHARD OF THE NIGHTBRINGER

12 POWER

NAME	M	WS	BS	S	T	W	A	Ld	Sv
C'tan Shard of the Nightbringer	8"	2+	2+	7	7	8	4	10	4+

The C'tan Shard of the Nightbringer is a single model which attacks with a gaze of death and the Scythe of the Nightbringer. Only one of this model may be included in your army.

WEAPON	RANGE	TYPE	S	AP	D	ABILITIES
Gaze of death	12"	Assault D6	*	-4	D3	This weapon wounds on a 2+, unless it is targeting a **VEHICLE**, in which case it wounds on a 6+.
Scythe of the Nightbringer	Melee	Melee	*	-4	D6	This weapon wounds on a 2+, unless it is targeting a **VEHICLE**, in which case it has a Strength characteristic of 7.

ABILITIES	**Necrodermis:** The C'tan Shard of the Nightbringer has a 4+ invulnerable save.	**Reality Unravels:** If the C'tan Shard of the Nightbringer is ever reduced to 0 wounds, roll a D6 before removing it from the battlefield; on a 4+ its necrodermis tears a hole in reality, and each unit within 3" suffers D3 mortal wounds.
	Powers of the C'tan: The C'tan Shard of the Nightbringer knows one Power of the C'tan (pg 85). It can use its Power of the C'tan in each of your Shooting phases.	

FACTION KEYWORDS	NECRONS, C'TAN SHARDS
KEYWORDS	CHARACTER, MONSTER, FLY, C'TAN SHARD OF THE NIGHTBRINGER

C'TAN SHARD OF THE DECEIVER

12 POWER

NAME	M	WS	BS	S	T	W	A	Ld	Sv
C'tan Shard of the Deceiver	8"	2+	2+	7	7	8	4	10	4+

The C'tan Shard of the Deceiver is a single model armed with star-god fists. Only one of this model may be included in your army.

WEAPON	RANGE	TYPE	S	AP	D	ABILITIES
Star-god fists	Melee	Melee	User	-4	3	-

ABILITIES	**Necrodermis:** The C'tan Shard of the Deceiver has a 4+ invulnerable save.	**Powers of the C'tan:** The C'tan Shard of the Deceiver knows one Power of the C'tan (pg 85). It can use its Power of the C'tan in each of your Shooting phases.
	Dread: Your opponent must add 1 to Morale tests for any enemy units within 12" of the C'tan Shard of the Deceiver.	**Reality Unravels:** If the C'tan Shard of the Deceiver is ever reduced to 0 wounds, roll a D6 before removing it from the battlefield; on a 4+ its necrodermis tears a hole in reality, and each unit within 3" suffers D3 mortal wounds.
	Grand Illusion: At the beginning of the first battle round, but before the first turn begins, you can remove the C'tan Shard of the Deceiver and/or up to D3 other friendly **NECRON** units from the battlefield, then set them up again more than 12" from any enemy models. If you do so, these units cannot charge in your first turn.	

FACTION KEYWORDS	NECRONS, C'TAN SHARDS
KEYWORDS	CHARACTER, MONSTER, FLY, C'TAN SHARD OF THE DECEIVER

GHOST ARK

8 POWER

NAME	M	WS	BS	S	T	W	A	Ld	Sv
Ghost Ark	*	6+	*	6	6	14	*	10	4+

A Ghost Ark is a single model equipped with two gauss flayer arrays.

DAMAGE
Some of this model's characteristics change as it suffers damage, as shown below:

REMAINING W	M	BS	A
8-14+	12"	3+	3
4-7	8"	4+	D3
1-3	4"	5+	1

WEAPON	RANGE	TYPE	S	AP	D	ABILITIES
Gauss flayer array	24"	Rapid Fire 5	4	-1	1	-

ABILITIES

Living Metal (pg 84)

Quantum Shielding: Each time this model suffers damage from an unsaved wound, roll a D6. If the result is less than the damage inflicted by the attack, the damage is ignored (e.g. if this model suffers 4 damage, if you then roll a 3 or less the damage is ignored).

Hovering: Distance and ranges are always measured to and from this model's hull, even though it has a base.

Explodes: If this model is reduced to 0 wounds, roll a D6 before removing it from the battlefield and before any units disembark. On a 6 it explodes, and each unit within 6" suffers D3 mortal wounds.

Repair Barge: You can make Reanimation Protocol rolls for any slain models from units embarked on a Ghost Ark, even though those units are not on the battlefield. Any models returned to the unit this way are added to the number of models embarked on the Ghost Ark – if any models cannot be returned because there is no more room on the Ghost Ark, they are not returned this turn. In addition, at the end of each of your Movement phases, you can make Reanimation Protocol rolls for any slain models from a single <Dynasty> Warriors unit within 3" of the Ghost Ark. You cannot use this ability on a unit that has been targeted with a resurrection orb this turn.

TRANSPORT	A Ghost Ark can transport 10 <Dynasty> Infantry models, which must be Warriors or Characters.
FACTION KEYWORDS	Necrons, <Dynasty>
KEYWORDS	Vehicle, Transport, Fly, Ghost Ark

NIGHT SCYTHE

8 POWER

NAME	M	WS	BS	S	T	W	A	Ld	Sv
Night Scythe	*	6+	*	6	6	12	*	10	3+

A Night Scythe is a single model equipped with two tesla destructors.

DAMAGE
Some of this model's characteristics change as it suffers damage, as shown below:

REMAINING W	M	BS	A
7-12+	20-60"	3+	3
4-6	20-40"	4+	D3
1-3	20-25"	5+	1

WEAPON	RANGE	TYPE	S	AP	D	ABILITIES
Tesla destructor	24"	Assault 4	7	0	1	Each hit roll of 6+ with this weapon causes 3 hits instead of 1.

ABILITIES

Living Metal (pg 84)

Airborne: This model cannot charge, can only be charged by units that can Fly, and can only attack or be attacked in the Fight phase by units that can Fly.

Hard to Hit: Your opponent must subtract 1 from hit rolls for attacks that target this model in the Shooting phase.

Supersonic: Each time this model moves, first pivot it on the spot up to 90° (this does not contribute to how far the model moves), and then move the model straight forwards. Note that it cannot pivot again after the initial pivot. When this model Advances, increase its Move characteristic by 20" until the end of the phase – do not roll a dice.

Crash and Burn: If this model is reduced to 0 wounds, roll a D6 before removing it from the battlefield. On a 6 it crashes in a fiery explosion and each unit within 6" suffers D3 mortal wounds.

Invasion Beams: When you set up this model, at the same time you can also set up any number of <Dynasty> Infantry units on their tomb world rather than setting them up on the battlefield. Before the Night Scythe moves in each of your Movement phases, a single unit that was set up on their tomb world can be beamed onto the battlefield by the Night Scythe. To do so, set up the unit so that it is wholly within 3" of the Night Scythe and more than 1" from the enemy. If all friendly Night Scythes and Monoliths are destroyed, any units still on the tomb world are considered to be slain.

FACTION KEYWORDS	Necrons, <Dynasty>
KEYWORDS	Vehicle, Fly, Night Scythe

DOOM SCYTHE

DAMAGE
Some of this model's characteristics change as it suffers damage, as shown below:

REMAINING W	M	BS	A
7-12+	20-60"	3+	3
4-6	20-40"	4+	D3
1-3	20-25"	5+	1

NAME	M	WS	BS	S	T	W	A	Ld	Sv
Doom Scythe	*	6+	*	6	6	12	*	10	3+

A Doom Scythe is a single model equipped with a death ray and two tesla destructors.

WEAPON	RANGE	TYPE	S	AP	D	ABILITIES
Death ray	24"	Heavy D3	10	-4	D6	-
Tesla destructor	24"	Assault 4	7	0	1	Each hit roll of 6+ with this weapon causes 3 hits instead of 1.

ABILITIES	
Living Metal (pg 84) **Airborne:** This model cannot charge, can only be charged by units that can **FLY**, and can only attack or be attacked in the Fight phase by units that can **FLY**. **Hard to Hit:** Your opponent must subtract 1 from hit rolls for attacks that target this model in the Shooting phase.	**Supersonic:** Each time this model moves, first pivot it on the spot up to 90° (this does not contribute to how far the model moves), and then move the model straight forwards. Note that it cannot pivot again after the initial pivot. When this model Advances, increase its Move characteristic by 20" until the end of the phase – do not roll a dice. **Crash and Burn:** If this model is reduced to 0 wounds, roll a D6 before removing it from the battlefield. On a 6 it crashes in a fiery explosion and each unit within 6" suffers D3 mortal wounds.

FACTION KEYWORDS	NECRONS, <DYNASTY>
KEYWORDS	**VEHICLE, FLY, DOOM SCYTHE**

CANOPTEK WRAITHS

NAME	M	WS	BS	S	T	W	A	Ld	Sv
Canoptek Wraith	12"	3+	3+	6	5	3	3	10	4+

This unit contains 3 Canoptek Wraiths. It may include up to 3 additional Canoptek Wraiths (**Power Rating +6**). Each model is equipped with vicious claws.

WEAPON	RANGE	TYPE	S	AP	D	ABILITIES
Particle caster	12"	Pistol 1	6	0	1	-
Transdimensional beamer	12"	Heavy D3	4	-3	1	Each time you roll a wound roll of 6+ for this weapon, the target suffers a mortal wound in addition to any other damage.
Vicious claws	Melee	Melee	User	-1	1	
Whip coils	Melee	Melee	User	0	1	If the bearer is slain in the Fight phase before it has made its attacks, leave the model where it is. When its unit is chosen to fight in that phase, it can do so as normal. Once it has done so, remove the model from the battlefield.

WARGEAR OPTIONS	• Any model may take a particle caster, transdimensional beamer or whip coils.
ABILITIES	**Wraith Form:** Models in this unit have a 3+ invulnerable save, and can move across models and terrain as if they were not there.
FACTION KEYWORDS	NECRONS, CANOPTEK, <DYNASTY>
KEYWORDS	**BEASTS, CANOPTEK WRAITHS**

CANOPTEK SCARABS

2 POWER

NAME	M	WS	BS	S	T	W	A	Ld	Sv
Canoptek Scarab Swarm	10"	3+	3+	3	3	3	4	10	6+

This unit contains 3 Canoptek Scarab Swarms. It may include up to 3 additional Canoptek Scarab Swarms (**Power Rating +2**) or up to 6 additional Canoptek Scarab Swarms (**Power Rating +4**). Each swarm is equipped with feeder mandibles.

WEAPON	RANGE	TYPE	S	AP	D	ABILITIES
Feeder mandibles	Melee	Melee	User	0	1	If the target's Toughness is higher than this attack's Strength, this weapon always wounds the target on a wound roll of 5+.

FACTION KEYWORDS	NECRONS, CANOPTEK, <DYNASTY>
KEYWORDS	SWARM, CANOPTEK SCARABS

TOMB BLADES

5 POWER

NAME	M	WS	BS	S	T	W	A	Ld	Sv
Tomb Blades	14"	3+	3+	4	5	2	1	10	4+

This unit contains 3 Tomb Blades. It can include up to 3 additional Tomb Blades (**Power Rating +5**) or up to 6 additional Tomb Blades (**Power Rating +10**). Each model is equipped with two gauss blasters.

WEAPON	RANGE	TYPE	S	AP	D	ABILITIES
Gauss blaster	24"	Rapid Fire 1	5	-2	1	-
Particle beamer	24"	Assault 3	6	0	1	-
Tesla carbine	24"	Assault 2	5	0	1	Each hit roll of 6+ with this weapon causes 3 hits instead of 1.

WARGEAR OPTIONS	• Any model may replace its two gauss blasters with two tesla carbines or a particle beamer. • Any model may take shieldvanes. • Any model may take a nebuloscope or a shadowloom.
ABILITIES	**Reanimation Protocols** (pg 84) **Nebuloscope:** Enemies attacked by a model with a nebuloscope do not receive a bonus to their save from being in cover.	**Shadowloom:** A model with a shadowloom has a 5+ invulnerable save. **Shieldvanes:** A model with shieldvanes has a Save characteristic of 3+.
FACTION KEYWORDS	NECRONS, <DYNASTY>
KEYWORDS	BIKER, FLY, TOMB BLADES

DESTROYERS

3 POWER

NAME	M	WS	BS	S	T	W	A	Ld	Sv
Destroyer	10"	3+	3+	4	5	3	2	10	3+
Heavy Destroyer	10"	3+	3+	4	5	3	2	10	3+

This unit contains 1 Destroyer. It can include up to 5 additional Destroyers (**Power Rating +3 per model**). If the unit contains at least three models, a Heavy Destroyer can take the place of a Destroyer.
• Each Destroyer is armed with a gauss cannon.
• The Heavy Destroyer is armed with a heavy gauss cannon.

WEAPON	RANGE	TYPE	S	AP	D	ABILITIES
Gauss cannon	24"	Heavy 2	5	-3	D3	-
Heavy gauss cannon	36"	Heavy 1	9	-4	D6	-

ABILITIES	**Reanimation Protocols** (pg 84) **Hardwired Hatred:** You can re-roll hit rolls of 1 for this unit.	**Repulsor Platform:** This unit can move and fire Heavy weapons without suffering the penalty to its hit rolls.
FACTION KEYWORDS	NECRONS, <DYNASTY>	
KEYWORDS	INFANTRY, FLY, DESTROYERS	

HEAVY DESTROYERS

4 POWER

NAME	M	WS	BS	S	T	W	A	Ld	Sv
Heavy Destroyer	10"	3+	3+	4	5	3	2	10	3+

This unit contains 1 Heavy Destroyer. It may include 1 additional Heavy Destroyer (**Power Rating +4**) or 2 additional Heavy Destroyers (**Power Rating +8**). Each model is equipped with a heavy gauss cannon.

WEAPON	RANGE	TYPE	S	AP	D	ABILITIES
Heavy gauss cannon	36"	Heavy 1	9	-4	D6	-

ABILITIES	Reanimation Protocols (pg 84)	Repulsor Platform: This unit can move and fire Heavy weapons without suffering the penalty to its hit rolls.
	Hardwired Hatred: You can re-roll hit rolls of 1 for this unit.	

FACTION KEYWORDS	NECRONS, <DYNASTY>
KEYWORDS	INFANTRY, FLY, HEAVY DESTROYERS

CANOPTEK SPYDERS

4 POWER

NAME	M	WS	BS	S	T	W	A	Ld	Sv
Canoptek Spyders	6"	4+	4+	6	6	4	4	10	3+

This unit contains 1 Canoptek Spyder. You may include 1 additional Canoptek Spyder (**Power Rating +4**) or 2 additional Canoptek Spyders (**Power Rating +8**). Each model is equipped with automaton claws.

WEAPON	RANGE	TYPE	S	AP	D	ABILITIES
Particle beamer	24"	Assault 3	6	0	1	-
Automaton claws	Melee	Melee	User	-2	D3	-

WARGEAR OPTIONS	• Any model may take a fabricator claw array. • Any model may take a gloom prism. • Any model may take two particle beamers.

ABILITIES	Fabricator Claw Array: At the end of your Movement phase a model equipped with a fabricator claw array can repair a single <DYNASTY> VEHICLE within 1". That model regains D3 wounds lost earlier in the battle. A model can only be repaired once per turn.	Scarab Hive: At the beginning of your turn, you can roll a D6 for each friendly <DYNASTY> Canoptek Scarabs unit that is below its starting number of models and within 6" of any Canoptek Spyders. On a roll of 1, one of those Canoptek Spyders units suffers D3 mortal wounds. On a 2+ one of the Canoptek Spyders units unleashes reinforcements: return a Canoptek Scarab Swarm to the depleted unit, in unit coherency and more than 1" from enemy models. If you cannot do this because there is no room to place the model, do not set it up.
	Gloom Prism: A model equipped with a gloom prism can attempt to deny one psychic power in each enemy Psychic phase.	

FACTION KEYWORDS	NECRONS, CANOPTEK, <DYNASTY>
KEYWORDS	MONSTER, CANOPTEK SPYDERS

19 POWER · MONOLITH

NAME	M	WS	BS	S	T	W	A	Ld	Sv
Monolith	*	6+	*	8	8	20	3	10	3+

A Monolith is a single model equipped with four gauss flux arcs and a particle whip.

WEAPON	RANGE	TYPE	S	AP	D	ABILITIES
Gauss flux arc	24"	Heavy 3	5	-2	1	-
Particle whip	24"	Heavy 6	8	-3	D3	

DAMAGE

Some of this model's characteristics change as it suffers damage, as shown below:

REMAINING W	M	BS	PORTAL OF EXILE
11-20+	6"	4+	4+
6-10	5"	5+	5+
1-5	4"	6+	6

ABILITIES

Living Metal (pg 84)

Death Descending: During deployment, you can set up a Monolith in the upper atmosphere instead of placing it on the battlefield. At the end of any of your Movement phases the Monolith can plummet to the battlefield – set it up anywhere on the battlefield that is more than 12" from any enemy models.

Portal of Exile: When an enemy unit (other than a **Monster** or **Vehicle**) charges this model, its portal of exile may activate. Roll a D6 and compare it to the value required on the damage table above. If the roll is successful, the charging unit suffers D6 mortal wounds.

Hovering: Distance and ranges are always measured to and from this model's hull, even though it has a base.

Floating Fortress: This model can move and fire Heavy weapons without suffering the penalty to its hit rolls.

Eternity Gate: When you set up this model, at the same time you can also set up any number of <**Dynasty**> **Infantry** units on their tomb world rather than setting them up on the battlefield. Before the Monolith moves in each of your Movement phases, a single unit that was set up on their tomb world can be transported onto the battlefield by the Monolith. To do so, set up the unit so that it is wholly within 3" of the Monolith and more than 1" from the enemy. If all friendly Night Scythes and Monoliths are destroyed, any units still on the tomb world are considered to be slain.

Explodes: If this model is reduced to 0 wounds, roll a D6 before removing it from the battlefield. On a 6 it explodes, and each unit within 6" suffers D6 mortal wounds.

FACTION KEYWORDS	**Necrons, <Dynasty>**
KEYWORDS	**Vehicle, Titanic, Fly, Monolith**

The Monolith is a terrifying symbol of Necron dominance, a floating fortress that calls forth rank after rank of soulless warriors.

7 POWER — ANNIHILATION BARGE

NAME	M	WS	BS	S	T	W	A	Ld	Sv
Annihilation Barge	12"	6+	3+	5	6	8	3	10	4+

An Annihilation Barge is a single model equipped with a gauss cannon and a twin tesla destructor.

WEAPON	RANGE	TYPE	S	AP	D	ABILITIES
Twin tesla destructor	24"	Assault 8	7	0	1	Each hit roll of 6+ with this weapon causes 3 hits instead of 1.
Gauss cannon	24"	Heavy 2	5	-3	D3	-
Tesla cannon	24"	Assault 3	6	0	1	Each hit roll of 6+ with this weapon causes 3 hits instead of 1.

WARGEAR OPTIONS	• This model may replace its gauss cannon with a tesla cannon.

ABILITIES	**Living Metal (pg 84)** **Quantum Shielding:** Each time this model suffers damage from an unsaved wound, roll a D6. If the result is less than the damage inflicted by the attack, the damage is ignored (e.g. if this model suffers 4 damage, if you then roll a 3 or less the damage is ignored).	**Explodes:** If this model is reduced to 0 wounds, roll a D6 before removing it from the battlefield. On a 6 it explodes, and each unit within 3" suffers a mortal wound.
FACTION KEYWORDS	NECRONS, <DYNASTY>	
KEYWORDS	VEHICLE, FLY, ANNIHILATION BARGE	

10 POWER — DOOMSDAY ARK

DAMAGE

Some of this model's characteristics change as it suffers damage, as shown below:

REMAINING W	M	BS	A
8-14+	12"	3+	3
4-7	8"	4+	D3
1-3	4"	5+	1

NAME	M	WS	BS	S	T	W	A	Ld	Sv
Doomsday Ark	*	6+	*	6	6	14	*	10	4+

A Doomsday Ark is a single model equipped with a doomsday cannon and two gauss flayer arrays.

WEAPON	RANGE	TYPE	S	AP	D	ABILITIES
Doomsday cannon	When attacking with this weapon, choose one of the profiles below.					
- Low power	24"	Heavy D3	8	-2	D3	-
- High power	72"	Heavy D3	10	-5	D6	A model can only fire the doomsday cannon at high power if it remained stationary in its preceding Movement phase. When targeting units with 10 or more models, change this weapon's Type to Heavy D6.
Gauss flayer array	24"	Rapid Fire 5	4	-1	1	-

ABILITIES	**Living Metal (pg 84)** **Explodes:** If this model is reduced to 0 wounds, roll a D6 before removing it from the battlefield. On a 6 it explodes, and each unit within 6" suffers D3 mortal wounds.	**Quantum Shielding:** Each time this model suffers damage from an unsaved wound, roll a D6. If the result is less than the damage inflicted by the attack, the damage is ignored (e.g. if this model suffers 4 damage, if you then roll a 3 or less the damage is ignored).
FACTION KEYWORDS	NECRONS, <DYNASTY>	
KEYWORDS	VEHICLE, FLY, DOOMSDAY ARK	

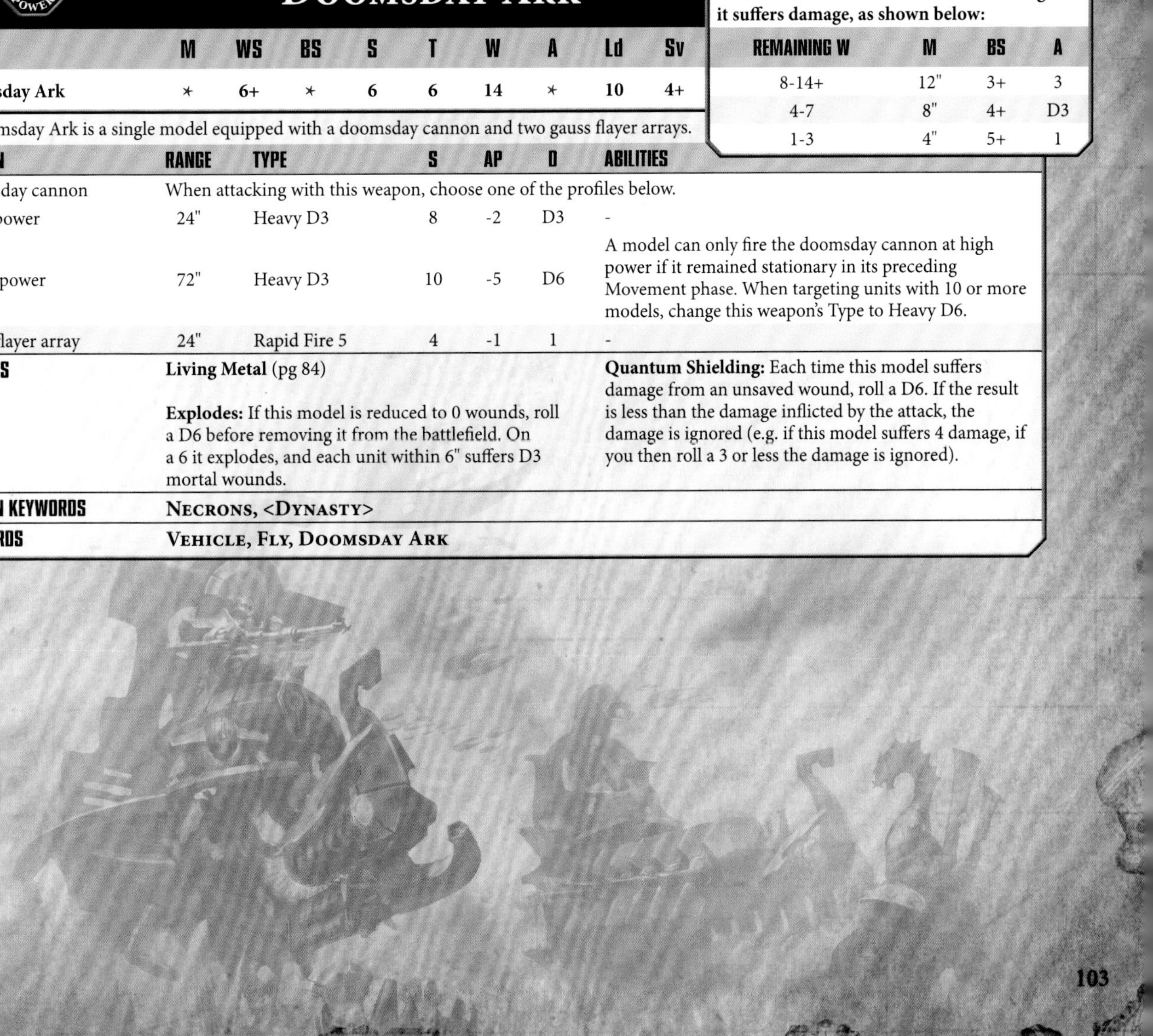

TRANSCENDENT C'TAN

12 POWER

NAME	M	WS	BS	S	T	W	A	Ld	Sv
Transcendent C'tan	8"	2+	2+	7	7	8	4	10	4+

A Transcendent C'tan is a single model armed with crackling tendrils.

WEAPON	RANGE	TYPE	S	AP	D	ABILITIES
Crackling tendrils	Melee	Melee	User	-4	D6	-

ABILITIES	
	Necrodermis: This model has a 4+ invulnerable save. **Reality Unravels:** If this model is ever reduced to 0 wounds, roll a D6 before removing it from the battlefield; on a 4+ its necrodermis tears a hole in reality, and each unit within 3" suffers D3 mortal wounds.
	Powers of the C'tan: This model knows one Power of the C'tan (pg 85). It can use its Power of the C'tan in each of your Shooting phases.
	Writhing Worldscape: Enemy units within 6" of this model do not receive a bonus to their save from being in cover.
FACTION KEYWORDS	NECRONS, C'TAN SHARDS
KEYWORDS	CHARACTER, MONSTER, FLY, TRANSCENDENT C'TAN

TESSERACT VAULT

24 POWER

NAME	M	WS	BS	S	T	W	A	Ld	Sv
Tesseract Vault	∗	6+	∗	8	7	28	3	10	3+

A Tesseract Vault is a single model equipped with four tesla spheres.

WEAPON	RANGE	TYPE	S	AP	D	ABILITIES
Tesla sphere	24"	Assault 5	7	0	1	Each hit roll of 6+ with this weapon causes 3 hits instead of 1.

ABILITIES	
	Living Metal (pg 84) **Vengeance of the Enchained:** If this model is reduced to 0 wounds, roll a D6 before removing it from the battlefield. On a 4+ the Transcendent C'tan contained within takes their vengeance, and each unit within 2D6" suffers D6 mortal wounds.
	Powers of the C'tan: This model knows three Powers of the C'tan (pg 85). It can use a number of Powers of the C'tan equal to the number in the damage table above in each of your Shooting phases.
FACTION KEYWORDS	NECRONS, C'TAN SHARDS, <DYNASTY>
KEYWORDS	VEHICLE, TITANIC, FLY, TESSERACT VAULT

DAMAGE

Some of this model's characteristics change as it suffers damage, as shown below:

REMAINING W	M	BS	POWERS OF THE C'TAN
15-28+	8"	3+	3
8-14	6"	4+	2
1-7	4"	5+	1

OBELISK

21 POWER

NAME	M	WS	BS	S	T	W	A	Ld	Sv
Obelisk	＊	6+	＊	8	8	24	3	10	3+

An Obelisk is a single model equipped with four tesla spheres.

WEAPON	RANGE	TYPE	S	AP	D	ABILITIES
Tesla sphere	24"	Assault 5	7	0	1	Each hit roll of 6+ with this weapon causes 3 hits instead of 1.

DAMAGE

Some of this model's characteristics change as it suffers damage, as shown below:

REMAINING W	M	BS	GRAVITY PULSE
13-24+	8"	3+	18"
7-12	6"	4+	12"
1-6	4"	5+	6"

ABILITIES	
	Living Metal (pg 84)
	Hovering Sentinel: During deployment, you can set up an Obelisk in the upper atmosphere instead of placing it on the battlefield. At the end of any of your Movement phases the Obelisk can plummet to the battlefield – set it up anywhere on the battlefield that is more than 12" from any enemy models.

Gravity Pulse: At the start of your Shooting phase, roll a dice for each enemy unit that can **FLY** and is within the distance specified on the damage table above. On a roll of 6, that unit suffers D3 mortal wounds.

Explodes: If this model is reduced to 0 wounds, roll a D6 before removing it from the battlefield. On a 6 it explodes, and each unit within 2D6" suffers D6 mortal wounds.

FACTION KEYWORDS	NECRONS, <DYNASTY>
KEYWORDS	VEHICLE, TITANIC, FLY, OBELISK

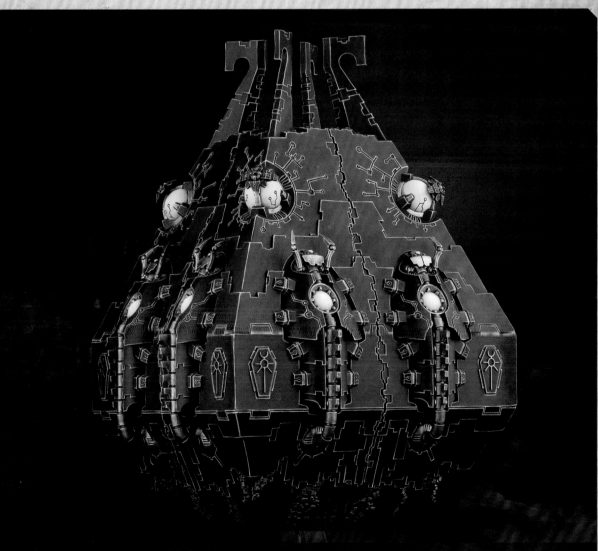

Necron Obelisks lash out with gravitic singularities to crush aircraft and shred enemies with arcs of deadly energy.

BATTLE-FORGED ARMIES

When picking a Battle-forged army for matched play, you will need to record the details of your army on a piece of paper (your Army Roster). Here we show one example of how you can do this; using several Detachment Rosters, at least one for each Detachment in your army, and the summarising main Army Roster itself. Over the page are blank rosters you can photocopy.

DETACHMENT ROSTERS

Each Detachment Roster details all the units it includes. Each unit has a small entry of its own where you can write down the name and type of unit, its Battlefield Role, the number of models it contains, and the weapons each model in the unit is equipped with. Details of how many models make up each unit and what weapons, options and upgrades each can take can be found on that unit's datasheet.

The points value of each unit's models and each individual weapon is then noted down by referencing the points lists in the appendix (pg 112-128), and added together to give a points cost for the unit. The points cost of the entire Detachment is simply then the sum of the points costs of its units. This can be noted down alongside other useful information, such as the number of Command Points (if any) the Detachment gives you (see the *Warhammer 40,000* rulebook for more on Command Points).

Unit Champions

Many units are led by a champion of some kind such as a Sergeant. Unit champions often have better characteristics and weapon options than the models they command. All the champions in this book have the same points cost as the others models in their unit.

Under-strength Units

Sometimes you may find that you do not have enough models to field a minimum-sized unit; if this is the case, you can still include one unit of that type in your army with as many models as you have available. In matched play games, you only pay the points for the models you actually have in an under-strength unit (and any weapons they are equipped with). An under-strength unit still takes up the appropriate slot in a Detachment.

ARMY ROSTER

Once you have filled in all of your Detachment Rosters, you can then fill out the main Army Roster. The name and points value of each Detachment is noted down here for reference. The total points cost of your army is the sum of all the Detachment points costs in your army plus any reinforcement points you have chosen to put aside (see below). The points cost of your army should not exceed the points limit you are using for the battle.

There are lots of other useful things to write down on your main Army Roster, such as who the army's Warlord is (this should be done at the start of the battle) and the number of Command Points available to your army. Remember that all Battle-forged armies start with 3 Command Points, but certain Detachments, and occasionally certain models, can change this total.

Reinforcement Points

Sometimes an ability will allow you to add units to your army, or replace units that have been destroyed. You must set aside some of your points in order to use these units. The points you set aside are called your reinforcement points, and need to be recorded on your army roster. Each time a unit is added to an army during battle, subtract the number of points the unit would cost from your pool of reinforcement points.

ARMY ROSTER

PLAYER NAME:	Alex Smith	ARMY FACTION:	Aeldari
ARMY NAME:	Warhost Starspear	WARLORD:	Yllathra Starspear

DETACHMENT NAME	TYPE	CPS	POINTS
Sons of Khaine	Battalion	3	684
Blades of Fate	Patrol	0	559
Blooded Serpents	Patrol	0	257

WARLORD TRAIT

FILL IN AT SET-UP:

Total Command Points:	6
Reinforcement Points:	0
TOTAL POINTS:	1500

DETACHMENT ROSTER

NAME:	Blades of Fate	TYPE:	Patrol

UNIT

UNIT TITLE:	BATTLEFIELD ROLE:	NO. OF MODELS:	POINTS (MODELS):
Farseer	HQ	1	106

WARGEAR:	POINTS (WARGEAR):
Shuriken pistol (0), witch blade (7)	7

	TOTAL POINTS (UNIT):	113

UNIT

UNIT TITLE:	BATTLEFIELD ROLE:	NO. OF MODELS:	POINTS (MODELS):
Guardian Defenders	Troops	10	80

WARGEAR:	POINTS (WARGEAR):
10 x shuriken catapults (0), 10 x sunburst grenades (0), Heavy Weapon Platform with a bright lance (5+20)	25

	TOTAL POINTS (UNIT):	105

UNIT

UNIT TITLE:	BATTLEFIELD ROLE:	NO. OF MODELS:	POINTS (MODELS):
Windriders	Fast Attack	6	120

WARGEAR:	POINTS (WARGEAR):
2 x twin shuriken catapults (20), 2 x scatter lasers (30), 2 x shuriken cannons (24)	74

	TOTAL POINTS (UNIT):	194

UNIT

UNIT TITLE:	BATTLEFIELD ROLE:	NO. OF MODELS:	POINTS (MODELS):
Wraithlord	Heavy Support	1	103

WARGEAR:	POINTS (WARGEAR):
Shuriken catapult (0), flamer (9), wraithbone fists (0), ghostglaive (10), Aeldari missile launcher (25)	44

	TOTAL POINTS (UNIT):	147

Total Points (Detachment):	559	Command Points:	0

NOTES: All units in the Blades of Fate Detachment are from the Saim-Hann Craftworld.

ARMY ROSTER

PLAYER NAME:		**ARMY FACTION:**	
ARMY NAME:		**WARLORD:**	

DETACHMENT NAME	TYPE	CPS	POINTS

WARLORD TRAIT

FILL IN AT SET-UP:

Total Command Points:	
Reinforcement Points:	
TOTAL POINTS:	

DETACHMENT ROSTER

NAME: | **TYPE:**

UNIT

UNIT TITLE:		BATTLEFIELD ROLE:	NO. OF MODELS:	POINTS (MODELS):
WARGEAR:				POINTS (WARGEAR):
			TOTAL POINTS (UNIT):	

UNIT

UNIT TITLE:		BATTLEFIELD ROLE:	NO. OF MODELS:	POINTS (MODELS):
WARGEAR:				POINTS (WARGEAR):
			TOTAL POINTS (UNIT):	

UNIT

UNIT TITLE:		BATTLEFIELD ROLE:	NO. OF MODELS:	POINTS (MODELS):
WARGEAR:				POINTS (WARGEAR):
			TOTAL POINTS (UNIT):	

UNIT

UNIT TITLE:		BATTLEFIELD ROLE:	NO. OF MODELS:	POINTS (MODELS):
WARGEAR:				POINTS (WARGEAR):
			TOTAL POINTS (UNIT):	

Total Points (Detachment): | **Command Points:**

NOTES:

CRAFTWORLDS POINTS VALUES

If you are playing a matched play game, or a game that uses a points limit, you can use the following lists to determine the total points cost of your army. Simply add together the points costs of all your models and the wargear they are equipped with to determine your army's total points value.

UNITS		
UNIT	MODELS PER UNIT	POINTS PER MODEL (Does not include wargear)
Autarch	1	65
Autarch Skyrunner	1	94
Autarch with Swooping Hawk Wings	1	85
Autarch with Warp Jump Generator	1	73
Crimson Hunter	1	143
Crimson Hunter Exarch	1	183
Dark Reapers	3-10	5
Dire Avengers	5-10	10
Falcon	1	174
Farseer	1	106
Farseer Skyrunner	1	154
Fire Dragons	5-10	7
Fire Prism	1	158
Guardian Defenders	10-20	8
- Heavy Weapon Platform	0-2	5
Hemlock Wraithfighter	1	211
Howling Banshees	5-10	12
Night Spinner	1	155
Rangers	5-10	20
Shining Spears	3-9	24
Spiritseer	1	66
Storm Guardians	8-24	7
Striking Scorpions	5-10	17
Swooping Hawks	5-10	10
Vaul's Wrath Support Battery	1-3	77
Vypers	1-3	64
War Walkers	1-3	61
Warlock	1	30
Warlock Conclave	2-10	30
Warlock Skyrunner	1	70
Warlock Skyrunner Conclave	2-10	70
Warp Spiders	5-10	14
Wave Serpent	1	107
Windriders	3-9	20
Wraithblades	5-10	29
Wraithguard	5-10	23
Wraithknight	1	402
Wraithlord	1	103

UNITS		
UNIT	MODELS PER UNIT	POINTS PER MODEL (Including wargear)
Asurmen	1	175
Avatar of Khaine	1	250
Baharroth	1	120
Eldrad Ulthran	1	180
Fuegan	1	160
Illic Nightspear	1	88
Jain Zar	1	146
Karandras	1	168
Maugan Ra	1	159
Prince Yriel	1	104

RANGED WEAPONS

WEAPON	POINTS PER WEAPON
Aeldari missile launcher	25
Avenger shuriken catapult	7
Bright lance	20
Chainsabres	16
D-cannon	50
D-scythe	22
Death spinner	8
Doomweaver	0
Dragon's breath flamer	17
Firepike	22
Flamer	9
Fusion gun	17
Fusion pistol	9
Hawk's talon	10
Heavy D-scythe	0
Heavy wraithcannon	50
Lasblaster	7
Laser lance	9
Melta bomb	0
Prism cannon	0
Pulse laser	0
Ranger long rifle	0
Reaper launcher	31
Scatter laser	15
Scorpion's claw	20
Shadow weaver	21
Shuriken cannon	12
Shuriken catapult	0
Shuriken pistol	0
Singing spear	14
Spinneret rifle	12
Star lance	12
Starcannon	30
Sunburst grenade	0
Suncannon	118
Sunrifle	11
Tempest launcher	38
Triskele	9
Twin Aeldari missile launcher	50
Twin bright lance	40
Twin scatter laser	30
Twin shuriken cannon	24
Twin shuriken catapult	10
Twin starcannon	60
Vibro cannon	20
Wraithcannon	17

MELEE WEAPONS

WEAPON	POINTS PER WEAPON
Aeldari blade	0
Biting blade	12
Chainsword	1
Diresword	4
Executioner	16
Ghostaxe	15
Ghostglaive	10
Ghostswords	6
Mirrorswords	5
Paragon blade	12
Power sword	4
Power glaive	4
Powerblades	4
Scorpion chainsword	2
Titanic feet	0
Titanic ghostglaive	65
Titanic wraithbone fists	0
Witchblade	7
Witch staff	0
Wraithbone fists	0
Wraithguard fists	0

OTHER WARGEAR

WARGEAR	POINTS PER ITEM
Banshee mask	0
Crystal targeting matrix	5
Forceshield	8
Mandiblasters	0
Scattershield	20
Shimmershield	20
Spirit stones	10
Star engines	10
Vectored engines	10

CRAFTWORLDS WARGEAR

RANGED WEAPONS

UNIT	RANGE	TYPE	S	AP	D	ABILITIES
Aeldari missile launcher	When attacking with this weapon, choose one of the profiles below.					
- Sunburst missile	48"	Heavy D6	4	-1	1	-
- Starshot missile	48"	Heavy 1	8	-2	D6	-
Avenger shuriken catapult	18"	Assault 2	4	0	1	Each time you make a wound roll of 6+ for this weapon, that hit is resolved with an AP of -3 instead of 0.
Bright lance	36"	Heavy 1	8	-4	D6	-
Chainsabres (shooting)	12"	Pistol 2	4	0	1	Each time you make a wound roll of 6+ for this weapon, that hit is resolved with an AP of -3 instead of 0.
Death spinner	12"	Assault 2	6	0	1	Each time you make a wound roll of 6+ for this weapon, that hit is resolved with an AP of -4 instead of 0.
Doomweaver	48"	Heavy 2D6	7	0	2	Wound rolls of 6+ for this weapon are resolved with AP -4 instead of AP 0. This weapon can target units that are not visible to the bearer.
Dragon's breath flamer	8"	Assault D6	5	-1	1	This weapon automatically hits its target.
D-cannon	24"	Heavy D3	10	-4	D6	-
D-scythe	8"	Assault D3	10	-4	1	When a unit fires its D-scythes, roll once for the number of attacks and use this for all D-scythes fired by the unit in this phase. This weapon automatically hits its target.
The Eye of Wrath	3"	Pistol D6	6	-2	1	This weapon can only be fired once per battle.
Firepike	18"	Assault 1	8	-4	D6	If the target is within half range of this weapon, roll two dice when inflicting damage with it and discard the lowest result.
Flamer	8"	Assault D6	4	0	1	This weapon automatically hits its target.
Fusion gun	12"	Assault 1	8	-4	D6	If the target is within half range of this weapon, roll two dice when inflicting damage with it and discard the lowest result.
Fusion pistol	6"	Pistol 1	8	-4	D6	If the target is within half range of this weapon, roll two dice when inflicting damage with it and discard the lowest result.
Hawk's talon	24"	Assault 4	5	0	1	-
Heavy D-scythe	16"	Assault D3	10	-4	2	This weapon automatically hits its target.
Heavy wraithcannon	36"	Assault 2	10	-4	D6	-
Lasblaster	24"	Rapid Fire 2	3	0	1	-
Laser lance (shooting)	6"	Assault 1	6	-4	2	-
The Maugetar (shooting)	When attacking with this weapon, choose one of the profiles below. Each time you make a wound roll of 6+ for this weapon, that hit is resolved with an AP of -3 instead of -1.					
- Shrieker	36"	Assault 1	6	-1	1	If an INFANTRY model is slain by an attack made with this weapon, its unit suffers D3 mortal wounds.
- Shuriken	36"	Assault 4	6	-1	1	-
Melta bomb	6"	Grenade 1	8	-4	D6	You can re-roll failed wound rolls for this weapon when targeting a VEHICLE.
Prism cannon	When attacking with this weapon, choose one of the profiles below.					
- Dispersed	60"	Heavy D6	6	-3	1	-
- Focused	60"	Heavy D3	9	-4	D3	-
- Lance	60"	Heavy 1	12	-5	D6	-
Pulse laser	48"	Heavy 2	8	-3	3	-
Ranger long rifle	36"	Heavy 1	4	0	1	This weapon may target a CHARACTER even if it is not the closest enemy unit. Each time you roll a wound roll of 6+ for this weapon, it inflicts a mortal wound in addition to any other damage.
Reaper launcher	When attacking with this weapon, choose one of the profiles below.					
- Starshot missile	48"	Heavy 1	8	-2	3	-
- Starswarm missile	48"	Heavy 2	5	-2	2	-
Scatter laser	36"	Heavy 4	6	0	1	-

RANGED WEAPONS

WEAPON	RANGE	TYPE	S	AP	D	ABILITIES
Scorpion's claw (shooting)	12"	Assault 2	4	0	1	Each time you make a wound roll of 6+ for this weapon, that hit is resolved with an AP of -3 instead of 0.
Shadow weaver	48"	Heavy D6	6	0	1	Each time you make a wound roll of 6+ for this weapon, that hit is resolved with an AP of -4 instead of 0. This weapon can target units that are not visible to the bearer.
Shuriken cannon	24"	Assault 3	6	0	1	Each time you make a wound roll of 6+ for this weapon, that hit is resolved with an AP of -3 instead of 0.
Shuriken catapult	12"	Assault 2	4	0	1	Each time you make a wound roll of 6+ for this weapon, that hit is resolved with an AP of -3 instead of 0.
Shuriken pistol	12"	Pistol 1	4	0	1	Each time you make a wound roll of 6+ for this weapon, that hit is resolved with an AP of -3 instead of 0.
Silent Death	12"	Assault 4	User	-3	1	-
Singing spear (shooting)	12"	Assault 1	9	0	D3	This weapon always wounds on a roll of 2+.
Spinneret rifle	18"	Rapid Fire 1	6	-4	1	-
Star lance (shooting)	6"	Assault 1	8	-4	2	-
Starcannon	36"	Heavy 2	6	-3	3	-
Sunburst grenade	6"	Grenade D6	4	-1	1	-
Suncannon	48"	Heavy 2D6	6	-3	D3	-
Sunrifle	24"	Assault 4	3	-2	1	If a unit suffers any unsaved wounds from this weapon, your opponent must subtract 1 from their hit rolls until the end of the turn.
Tempest launcher	36"	Heavy 2D6	4	-2	1	This weapon can target units that are not visible to the bearer.
Triskele (shooting)	12"	Assault 3	3	-2	1	-
Twin Aeldari missile launcher		When attacking with this weapon, choose one of the profiles below.				
- Sunburst missile	48"	Heavy 2D6	4	-1	1	-
- Starshot missile	48"	Heavy 2	8	-2	D6	-
Twin bright lance	36"	Heavy 2	8	-4	D6	-
Twin scatter laser	36"	Heavy 8	6	0	1	-
Twin shuriken cannon	24"	Assault 6	6	0	1	Each time you make a wound roll of 6+ for this weapon, that hit is resolved with an AP of -3 instead of 0.
Twin shuriken catapult	12"	Assault 4	4	0	1	Each time you make a wound roll of 6+ for this weapon, that hit is resolved with an AP of -3 instead of 0.
Twin starcannon	36"	Heavy 4	6	-3	3	-
Vibro cannon	48"	Heavy 1	7	-1	D3	For each vibro cannon that has already been fired at the same target in this phase, improve the AP of this weapon by 1 (to a maximum of -3) and add 1 to the wound rolls for this weapon (to a maximum of +2). For example, if a firing model is the third to target the same unit with a vibro cannon, its AP is -3 and you add 2 to its wound rolls.
Voidbringer	48"	Heavy 1	4	-3	D3	This weapon can target an enemy CHARACTER even if they are not the closest enemy unit. This weapon wounds on a 2+, unless it is targeting a VEHICLE. Each time you roll a wound roll of 6+ for this weapon, it inflicts a mortal wound in addition to any other damage.
The Wailing Doom (shooting)	12"	Assault 1	8	-4	D6	Roll two dice when inflicting damage with this weapon and discard the lowest result.
Wraithcannon	12"	Assault 1	10	-4	D6	-

MELEE WEAPONS

WEAPON	RANGE	TYPE	S	AP	D	ABILITIES
Aeldari blade	Melee	Melee	User	0	1	You can re-roll failed hit rolls for this weapon.
Biting blade	Melee	Melee	+2	-1	2	-
Blade of Destruction	Melee	Melee	User	-3	D3	You can re-roll failed wound rolls for this weapon.
Chainsabres (melee)	Melee	Melee	+1	0	1	Each time the bearer fights, it can make 1 additional attack with this weapon.
Chainsword	Melee	Melee	User	0	1	Each time the bearer fights, it can make 1 additional attack with this weapon.
Diresword	Melee	Melee	User	2	1	Each time you make a wound roll of 6+ for this weapon, the target suffers a mortal wound in addition to any other damage.
Executioner	Melee	Melee	+2	-3	D3	When attacking with this weapon, you must subtract 1 from the hit roll.
Fire Axe	Melee	Melee	User	-4	D3	-
Ghostaxe	Melee	Melee	+2	-3	D3	When attacking with this weapon, you must subtract 1 from the hit roll.
Ghostglaive	Melee	Melee	+2	-4	D6	-
Ghostswords	Melee	Melee	+1	-2	1	Each time the bearer fights, it can make 1 additional attack with this weapon.
Laser lance (melee)	Melee	Melee	User	-4	2	If the bearer charged this turn, attacks with this weapon are made at Strength 6.
The Maugetar (scythe blade)	Melee	Melee	+2	-2	D3	-
Mirrorswords	Melee	Melee	User	-2	1	You can re-roll failed hit rolls in the Fight phase for this weapon.
Paragon blade	Melee	Melee	User	-4	1	You can re-roll failed hit and wound rolls for this weapon.
Power glaive	Melee	Melee	+1	-2	1	-
Power sword	Melee	Melee	User	-3	1	-
Powerblades	Melee	Melee	User	-2	1	Each time the bearer fights, it can make 1 additional attack with this weapon.
Scorpion chainsword	Melee	Melee	+1	0	1	-
Scorpion's claw (melee)	Melee	Melee	x2	-3	D3	When attacking with this weapon, you must subtract 1 from the hit roll.
The Shining Blade	Melee	Melee	User	-2	D3	If a unit suffers any unsaved wounds from this weapon, your opponent must subtract 1 from that unit's hit rolls until the end of the turn.
Singing spear (melee)	Melee	Melee	User	0	D3	This weapon always wounds on a roll of 2+.
The Spear of Twilight	Melee	Melee	User	-2	D3	This weapon always wounds on a roll of 2+.
Staff of Ulthamar	Melee	Melee	+2	-2	D3	-
Star lance (melee)	Melee	Melee	User	-4	2	If the bearer charged this turn, attacks with this weapon are made at Strength 8.
The Sword of Asur	Melee	Melee	+1	-3	D3	Each time you make a wound roll of 6+ for this weapon, the target suffers D3 mortal wounds in addition to any other damage.
Titanic feet	Melee	Melee	User	-2	D3	When you make an attack with this weapon, roll 3 dice instead of 1.
Titanic ghostglaive	Melee	Melee	x2	-4	6	-
Titanic wraithbone fists	Melee	Melee	User	-3	D6	-
Triskele (melee)	Melee	Melee	User	-2	1	-
The Wailing Doom (melee)	Melee	Melee	+2	-4	D6	Roll two dice when inflicting damage with this weapon and discard the lowest result.
Witch staff	Melee	Melee	User	0	2	This weapon always wounds on a roll of 2+.
Witchblade	Melee	Melee	User	0	D3	This weapon always wounds on a roll of 2+.
Wraithbone fists	Melee	Melee	User	-3	3	-
Wraithguard fists	Melee	Melee	User	-1	D3	-

OTHER WARGEAR

VEHICLE EQUIPMENT	EFFECT
Crystal targeting matrix	A model with a crystal targeting matrix does not suffer the penalty for firing a Heavy weapon after moving when targeting the closest enemy unit.
Spirit stones	Roll a D6 each time a model with spirit stones suffers an unsaved wound or mortal wound: on a 6 the wound is ignored.
Star engines	When a model with star engines Advances, add 2D6" to that model's Move characteristic for that Movement phase instead of D6".
Vectored engines	If a model with vectored engines Advances, your opponent must subtract 1 from all hit rolls for ranged weapons that target it until your next Movement phase.

DRUKHARI POINTS VALUES

If you are playing a matched play game, or a game that uses a points limit, you can use the following lists to determine the total points cost of your army. Simply add together the points costs of all your models and the wargear they are equipped with to determine your army's total points value.

UNITS

UNIT	MODELS PER UNIT	POINTS PER MODEL (Does not include wargear)
Archon	1	54
Beastmaster	1	56
Clawed Fiends	1-6	32
Cronos	1-3	102
Grotesques	3-10	31
Haemonculus	1	75
Hekatrix Bloodbrides	5-20	13
Hellions	5-20	17
Incubi	5-10	18
Kabalite Trueborn	5-20	11
Kabalite Warriors	5-20	7
Khymerae	2-12	10
Lhamaean	1	32
Mandrakes	5-10	19
Medusae	1	28
Raider	1	95
Ravager	1	95
Razorwing Jetfighter	1	115
Razorwing Flocks	1-12	7
Reavers	3-12	30
Scourges	5-10	14
Sslyth	1	44
Succubus	1	72
Talos	1-3	88
Ur-Ghul	1	30
Venom	1	65
Voidraven	1	169
Wracks	5-10	10
Wyches	5-20	9

RANGED WEAPONS

WEAPON	POINTS PER WEAPON
Baleblast	0
Blast pistol	10
Blaster	15
Dark lance	20
Dark scythe	0
Darklight grenade	0
Disintegrator cannon	30
Eyeburst	0
Haywire blaster	12
Heat lance	25
Hexrifle	11
Liquifier gun	13
Ossefactor	13
Phantasm grenade launcher	3
Razorwing missiles	0
Shardcarbine	0
Shredder	8
Spirit syphon	0
Spirit vortex	13
Splinter cannon	15
Splinter pistol	0
Splinter pods	0
Splinter rifle	0
Stinger pistol	7
Stinger pod	26
Twin liquifier gun	26
Twin splinter rifle	0
Void lance	0
Voidraven missiles	25

UNITS

UNIT	MODELS PER UNIT	POINTS PER MODEL (Including wargear)
Drazhar	1	140
Lelith Hesperax	1	125
Urien Rakarth	1	112

MELEE WEAPONS

WEAPON	POINTS PER WEAPON
Agoniser	4
Archite glaive	0
Beastmaster's scourge	4
Bladevanes	0
Bludgeoning fists	0
Chain-flails	3
Claws and talons	0
Demiklaives	8
Electrocorrosive whip	8
Flesh gauntlet	6
Glimmersteel blade	0
Haemonculus tools	1
Hekatarii blade	0
Hellglaive	0
Huskblade	10
Hydra gauntlets	4
Ichor injector	5
Impaler	5
Klaive	0
Macro-scalpel	4
Mindphase gauntlet	4
Monstrous cleaver	3
Power lance	4
Power sword	4
Razorflails	4
Scissorhand	8
Shaimeshi blade	0
Shardnet and impaler	5
Shock prow	1
Spirit-leech tentacles	0
Sslyth battle-blade	0
Stunclaw	7
Venom blade	5

OTHER WARGEAR

WARGEAR	POINTS PER ITEM
Cluster caltrops	5
Grav-talon	5

DRUKHARI WARGEAR

RANGED WEAPONS

WEAPON	RANGE	TYPE	S	AP	D	ABILITIES
Baleblast	18"	Assault 2	4	-1	1	Each time you roll a wound roll of 6+ for this weapon, the target suffers a mortal wound in addition to any other damage.
Blast pistol	6"	Pistol 1	8	-4	D3	-
Blaster	18"	Assault 1	8	-4	D3	-
Casket of Flensing	12"	Assault 2D6	3	-2	1	This weapon can only be fired once per battle.
Dark lance	36"	Heavy 1	8	-4	D6	Change the weapon's Type from Heavy to Assault if it is equipped on a **VEHICLE**.
Dark scythe	24"	Assault D3	8	-4	D3	-
Darklight grenade	6"	Grenade D6	4	-1	1	-
Disintegrator cannon	36"	Assault 3	5	-3	2	-
Eyeburst	9"	Assault 4	4	-2	1	-
Haywire blaster	24"	Assault 1	4	-1	1	If the target is a **VEHICLE** and you roll a wound roll of 4+ for this weapon, the target suffers a mortal wound in addition to any other damage. If the wound roll is 6+, inflict D3 mortal wounds instead of 1.
Heat lance	18"	Assault 1	6	-5	D6	If the target is within half range of this weapon, roll two dice when inflicting damage with it and discard the lowest result.
Hexrifle	36"	Heavy 1	4	-1	1	This weapon may target a **CHARACTER** even if it is not the closest enemy unit. Each time you roll a wound roll of 6+ for this weapon, the target suffers a mortal wound in addition to any other damage.
Liquifier gun	8"	Assault D6	3	-D3	1	Each time this weapon is fired, roll a D3 to determine its AP for those attacks. For example, if you rolled a 1, this weapon would have an AP of -1. This weapon automatically hits its target.
Ossefactor	24"	Assault 1	*	-3	1	This weapon wounds on a 2+, unless it is targeting a **VEHICLE**, in which case it wounds on a 6+. If a model is slain by this weapon, the model's unit immediately suffers a mortal wound on a D6 roll of 4+.
Phantasm grenade launcher	18"	Assault D3	1	0	1	If a unit is hit by one or more phantasm grenade launchers, subtract one from its Leadership until the end of the turn.
Razorwing missiles	When attacking with this weapon, choose one of the profiles below.					
- Monoscythe missile	48"	Assault D6	6	0	2	-
- Necrotoxin missile	48"	Assault 6	*	0	1	When you use this profile, this weapon wounds on a 2+, unless it is targeting a **VEHICLE**, in which case it wounds on a 6+.
- Shatterfield missile	48"	Assault D6	7	-1	1	When you use this profile, you can re-roll failed wound rolls for this weapon.
Shardcarbine	18"	Assault 3	*	0	1	This weapon wounds on a 4+, unless it is targeting a **VEHICLE**, in which case it wounds on a 6+.
Shredder	12"	Assault D3	6	0	1	When attacking a unit of **INFANTRY**, you can re-roll failed wound rolls for this weapon.
Spirit syphon	8"	Assault D6	3	-2	1	This weapon automatically hits its target. Any attacks with a wound roll of 6+ for this weapon have a Damage characteristic of D3 instead of 1.
Spirit vortex	18"	Assault D6	3	-2	1	Any attacks with a wound roll of 6+ for this weapon have a Damage characteristic of D3 instead of 1.
Splinter cannon	36"	Rapid Fire 3	*	0	1	This weapon wounds on a 4+, unless it is targeting a **VEHICLE**, in which case it wounds on a 6+.
Splinter pistol	12"	Pistol 1	*	0	1	This weapon wounds on a 4+, unless it is targeting a **VEHICLE**, in which case it wounds on a 6+.
Splinter pods	18"	Assault 2	*	0	1	This weapon wounds on a 4+, unless it is targeting a **VEHICLE**, in which case it wounds on a 6+.
Splinter rifle	24"	Rapid Fire 1	*	0	1	This weapon wounds on a 4+, unless it is targeting a **VEHICLE**, in which case it wounds on a 6+.
Stinger pistol	12"	Pistol 1	*	0	1	This weapon wounds on a 4+, unless it is targeting a **VEHICLE**, in which case it wounds on a 6+.
Stinger pod	24"	Assault 2D6	5	0	1	-

RANGED WEAPONS

WEAPON	RANGE	TYPE	S	AP	D	ABILITIES
Twin liquifier gun	8"	Assault 2D6	3	-D3	1	Each time this weapon is fired, roll a D3 to determine its AP for those attacks. For example, if you rolled a 1, this weapon would have an AP of -1. This weapon automatically hits its target.
Twin splinter rifle	24"	Rapid Fire 2	*	0	1	This weapon wounds on a 4+, unless it is targeting a VEHICLE, in which case it wounds on a 6+.
Void lance	36"	Assault 1	9	-4	D6	-
Voidraven missiles	When attacking with this weapon, choose one of the profiles below.					
- Implosion missile	48"	Assault D3	6	-3	1	-
- Shatterfield missile	48"	Assault D6	7	-1	1	You can re-roll failed wound rolls for this weapon.

MELEE WEAPONS

WEAPON	RANGE	TYPE	S	AP	D	ABILITIES
Agoniser	Melee	Melee	*	-2	1	This weapon wounds on a 4+, unless it is targeting a VEHICLE, in which case it wounds on a 6+.
Archite glaive	Melee	Melee	+2	-3	1	When attacking with this weapon, you must subtract 1 from the hit roll.
Beastmaster's scourge	Melee	Melee	+1	0	1	-
Bladevanes	Melee	Melee	4	-1	1	-
Bludgeoning fists	Melee	Melee	User	-1	2	-
Chain-flails	Melee	Melee	User	0	1	You can re-roll failed wound rolls for this weapon.
Claws and talons	Melee	Melee	User	0	1	-
Demiklaives	Each time this model fights, choose one of the profiles below.					
- Single blade	Melee	Melee	+1	-3	1	-
- Dual blades	Melee	Melee	User	-2	1	A model attacking with dual blades can make 2 additional attacks with them each time it fights.
Electrocorrosive whip	Melee	Melee	*	-2	2	This weapon wounds on a 4+, unless it is targeting a VEHICLE, in which case it wounds on a 6+.
Flesh gauntlet	Melee	Melee	*	0	1	This weapon wounds on a 4+, unless it is targeting a VEHICLE, in which case it wounds on a 6+. Each time you roll a wound roll of 6+ for this weapon, other than against VEHICLES, the target suffers a mortal wound in addition to any other damage.
Glimmersteel blade	Melee	Melee	User	0	1	Each time the bearer fights, it can make 1 additional attack with this weapon.
Haemonculus tools	Melee	Melee	*	0	1	This weapon wounds on a 4+, unless it is targeting a VEHICLE, in which case it wounds on a 6+.
Hekatarii blade	Melee	Melee	User	0	1	Each time the bearer fights, it can make 1 additional attack with this weapon.
Hellglaive	Melee	Melee	+1	0	2	-
Huskblade	Melee	Melee	User	-2	D3	-
Hydra gauntlets	Melee	Melee	User	-1	1	Each time the bearer fights, it can make 1 additional attack with this weapon. You can re-roll failed wound rolls for this weapon.
Ichor injector	Melee	Melee	User	0	1	The bearer can make a maximum of one attack with the ichor injector each turn (any remaining attacks must be made with a different melee weapon). You can re-roll wound rolls for this weapon. Each time you roll a wound roll of 6+ for this weapon, the target suffers D3 mortal wounds in addition to any other damage.
Impaler	Melee	Melee	User	-1	2	-
Klaive	Melee	Melee	+1	-3	1	-
Macro-scalpel	Melee	Melee	User	-1	2	A model armed with a macro-scalpel can make one additional close combat attack with it each time it fights. A model armed with two macro-scalpels can make two additional close combat attacks with them each time it fights.
Mane of barbs and hooks	Melee	Melee	User	0	1	Each time the bearer fights, it can make 2 additional attacks with this weapon.
Mindphase gauntlet	Melee	Melee	User	0	2	-

MELEE WEAPONS

WEAPON	RANGE	TYPE	S	AP	D	ABILITIES
Monstrous cleaver	Melee	Melee	User	-1	1	Each time the bearer fights, it can make 1 additional attack with this weapon.
Penetrating blade	Melee	Melee	User	-4	1	A model armed with two penetrating blades can make 1 additional attack with them each time it fights.
Power lance	Melee	Melee	+2	-1	1	-
Power sword	Melee	Melee	User	-3	1	-
Razorflails	Melee	Melee	User	-1	1	Each time the bearer fights, it can make 1 additional attack with this weapon. You can re-roll failed hit rolls for this weapon.
Scissorhand	Melee	Melee	*	-1	1	This weapon wounds on a 4+, unless it is targeting a **VEHICLE**, in which case it wounds on a 6+. Each time the bearer fights, it can make 1 additional attack with this weapon.
Shaimeshi blade	Melee	Melee	*	0	1	This weapon wounds on a 2+, unless it is targeting a **VEHICLE**, in which case it wounds on a 6+. Each time you roll a wound roll of 6+ for this weapon, other than against a **VEHICLE**, the target suffers a mortal wound in addition to any other damage.
Shardnet and impaler	Melee	Melee	User	-1	2	-
Shock prow	Melee	Melee	User	-1	1	You can make a maximum of one close combat attack with a shock prow each turn (any remaining attacks must be made with a different melee weapon). If the bearer charged this turn, successful attacks with this weapon have a Damage characteristic of D3 instead of 1.
Spirit-leech tentacles	Melee	Melee	User	-1	1	Any attacks with a wound roll of 6+ for this weapon have a Damage characteristic of D3 instead of 1.
Sslyth battle-blade	Melee	Melee	User	-1	1	-
Stunclaw	Melee	Melee	+1	0	1	Each time you roll a wound roll of 6+ for this weapon, the target suffers a mortal wound in addition to any other damage.
Venom blade	Melee	Melee	*	0	1	This weapon wounds on a 2+, unless it is targeting a **VEHICLE**, in which case it wounds on a 6+.

HARLEQUINS POINTS VALUES

If you are playing a matched play game, or a game that uses a points limit, you can use the following lists to determine the total points cost of your army. Simply add together the points costs of all your models and the wargear they are equipped with to determine your army's total points value.

UNITS

UNIT	MODELS PER UNIT	POINTS PER MODEL (Does not include wargear)
Death Jester	1	75
Shadowseer	1	134
Skyweavers	2-6	35
Solitaire	1	94
Starweaver	1	79
Troupe	5-12	15
Troupe Master	1	59
Voidweavers	1-3	68

MELEE WEAPONS

WEAPON	POINTS PER WEAPON
Harlequin's blade	1
Harlequin's caress	9
Harlequin's embrace	6
Harlequin's kiss	14
Miststave	0
Power sword	4
Zephyrglaive	11

RANGED WEAPONS

WEAPON	POINTS PER WEAPON
Fusion pistol	9
Hallucinogen grenade launcher	0
Haywire cannon	14
Neuro disruptor	10
Prismatic cannon	20
Prismatic grenades	0
Shrieker cannon	0
Shuriken cannon	10
Shuriken pistol	0
Star bolas	0

HARLEQUINS WARGEAR

RANGED WEAPONS

WEAPON	RANGE	TYPE	S	AP	D	ABILITIES
Fusion pistol	6"	Pistol 1	8	-4	D6	If the target is within half range of this weapon, roll two dice when inflicting damage with it and discard the lowest result.
Hallucinogen grenade launcher	18"	Assault 1	*	*	*	Roll 2D6 if a unit is hit by this weapon – if the roll is equal to or greater than the target unit's Leadership, then it suffers D3 mortal wounds.
Haywire cannon	24"	Heavy D3	4	-1	1	If the target is a **VEHICLE** and you roll a wound roll of 4+ for this weapon, the target suffers 1 mortal wound in addition to any other damage. If the wound roll is 6+, the target suffers D3 mortal wounds instead of 1.
Neuro disruptor	12"	Pistol 1	3	-3	D3	This weapon has a Damage of 1 against **VEHICLE** targets.
Prismatic cannon	When attacking with this weapon, choose one of the profiles below.					
- Dispersed	24"	Heavy D6	4	-2	1	-
- Focused	24"	Heavy D3	6	-3	D3	-
- Lance	24"	Heavy 1	8	-4	D6	-
Prismatic grenade	6"	Grenade D6	4	-1	1	-
Shrieker cannon	When attacking with this weapon, choose one of the profiles below. Each time you make a wound roll of 6+ for this weapon, that hit is resolved with an AP of -3 instead of 0.					
- Shrieker	24"	Assault 1	6	0	1	If an **INFANTRY** model is slain by an attack made with this weapon, then its unit suffers D3 mortal wounds.
- Shuriken	24"	Assault 3	6	0	1	
Shuriken cannon	24"	Assault 3	6	0	1	Each time you make a wound roll of 6+ for this weapon, that hit is resolved with an AP of -3 instead of 0.
Shuriken pistol	12"	Pistol 1	4	0	1	Each time you make a wound roll of 6+ for this weapon, that hit is resolved with an AP of -3 instead of 0.
Star bolas	12"	Grenade D3	6	-3	1	-

MELEE WEAPONS

WEAPON	RANGE	TYPE	S	AP	D	ABILITIES
Harlequin's blade	Melee	Melee	User	0	1	-
Harlequin's caress	Melee	Melee	5	-2	1	-
Harlequin's embrace	Melee	Melee	4	-3	1	-
Harlequin's kiss	Melee	Melee	4	-1	D3	-
Miststave	Melee	Melee	+2	-1	D3	-
Power sword	Melee	Melee	User	-3	1	-
Zephyrglaive	Melee	Melee	+1	-2	2	-

YNNARI POINTS VALUES

If you are playing a matched play game, or a game that uses a points limit, you can use the following lists to determine the total points cost of your army. Simply add together the points costs of all your models and the wargear they are equipped with to determine your army's total points value.

UNITS		
UNIT	**MODELS PER UNIT**	**POINTS PER MODEL** (Including wargear)
The Visarch	1	141
The Yncarne	1	337
Yvraine	1	132

YNNARI WARGEAR

MELEE WEAPONS						
WEAPON	**RANGE**	**TYPE**	**S**	**AP**	**D**	**ABILITIES**
Asu-var, the Sword of Silent Screams	Melee	Melee	+2	-3	D3	Enemy units that suffer any unsaved wounds from this weapon subtract 1 from their Leadership until the end of the turn.
Kha-vir, the Sword of Sorrows	Melee	Melee	+1	-2	D3	-
Vilith-zhar, the Sword of Souls	Melee	Melee	User	-4	D6	You can re-roll failed wound rolls for this weapon.

NECRONS POINTS VALUES

If you are playing a matched play game, or a game that uses a points limit, you can use the following lists to determine the total points cost of your army. Simply add together the points costs of all your models and the wargear they are equipped with to determine your army's total points value.

UNITS

UNIT	MODELS PER UNIT	POINTS PER MODEL (Does not include wargear)
Annihilation Barge	1	133
Canoptek Scarabs	3-9	13
Canoptek Spyders	1-3	76
Canoptek Wraiths	3-6	38
Catacomb Command Barge	1	138
Cryptek	1	86
Deathmarks	5-10	20
Destroyer Lord	1	124
Destroyers	1-6	43
Doom Scythe	1	220
Doomsday Ark	1	203
Flayed Ones	5-20	21
Ghost Ark	1	170
Heavy Destroyers	1-3	43
Immortals	5-10	8
Lord	1	73
Lychguard	5-10	19
Monolith	1	381
Night Scythe	1	174
Obelisk	1	426
Overlord	1	101
Tesseract Vault	1	496
Tomb Blades	3-9	24
Transcendent C'tan	1	232
Triarch Praetorians	5-10	25
Triarch Stalker	1	117
Warriors	10-20	12

UNITS

UNIT	MODELS PER UNIT	POINTS PER MODEL (Including wargear)
Anrakyr the Traveller	1	167
C'tan Shard of the Deceiver	1	225
C'tan Shard of the Nightbringer	1	230
Illuminor Szeras	1	143
Imotekh the Stormlord	1	228
Nemesor Zahndrekh	1	180
Orikan the Diviner	1	143
Trazyn the Infinite	1	139
Vargard Obyron	1	151

RANGED WEAPONS

WEAPON	POINTS PER WEAPON
Death ray	0
Doomsday cannon	0
Gauss blaster	9
Gauss cannon	20
Gauss flayer	0
Gauss flayer array	0
Gauss flux arc	0
Heat ray	54
Heavy gauss cannon	32
Particle beamer	10
Particle caster	4
Particle shredder	41
Particle whip	0
Rod of covenant	10
Staff of light	18
Synaptic disintegrator	0
Tesla cannon	13
Tesla carbine	9
Tesla destructor	0
Tesla sphere	0
Transdimensional beamer	14
Twin heavy gauss cannon	64
Twin tesla destructor	0

MELEE WEAPONS

WEAPON	POINTS PER WEAPON
Automaton claws	0
Crackling tendrils	0
Feeder mandibles	0
Flayer claws	0
Hyperphase sword	3
Massive forelimbs	0
Vicious claws	0
Voidblade	6
Warscythe	11
Whip coils	9

OTHER WARGEAR

WARGEAR	POINTS PER ITEM
Dispersion shield	15
Fabricator claw array	8
Gloom prism	5
Nebuloscope	3
Phylactery	15
Resurrection orb	35
Shadowloom	5
Shieldvanes	6

NECRONS WARGEAR

RANGED WEAPONS

WEAPON	RANGE	TYPE	S	AP	D	ABILITIES
Death ray	24"	Heavy D3	10	-4	D6	-
Doomsday cannon	When attacking with this weapon, choose one of the profiles below.					
- Low power	24"	Heavy D3	8	-2	D3	-
- High power	72"	Heavy D3	10	-5	D6	A model can only fire the doomsday cannon at high power if it remained stationary in its preceding Movement phase. When targeting units with 10 or more models, change this weapon's Type to Heavy D6.
Eldritch Lance (shooting)	36"	Assault 1	8	-4	D6	-
Gauntlet of fire	8"	Assault D6	4	0	1	This weapon automatically hits its target.
Gauss blaster	24"	Rapid Fire 1	5	-2	1	-
Gauss cannon	24"	Heavy 2	5	-3	D3	-
Gauss flayer	24"	Rapid Fire 1	4	-1	1	-
Gauss flayer array	24"	Rapid Fire 5	4	-1	1	-
Gauss flux arc	24"	Heavy 3	5	-2	1	-
Gaze of death	12"	Assault D6	*	-4	D3	This weapon wounds on a 2+, unless it is targeting a VEHICLE, in which case it wounds on a 6+.
Heat ray	When attacking with this weapon, choose one of the profiles below.					
- Dispersed	8"	Heavy D6	5	-1	1	When you use this profile, this weapon automatically hits its target.
- Focused	24"	Heavy 2	8	-4	D6	When you use this profile, if the target is within half range, roll two dice when inflicting damage with it and discard the lowest result.
Heavy gauss cannon	36"	Heavy 1	9	-4	D6	-
Particle beamer	24"	Assault 3	6	0	1	-
Particle caster	12"	Pistol 1	6	0	1	-
Particle shredder	24"	Heavy 6	7	-1	D3	-
Particle whip	24"	Heavy 6	8	-2	D3	-
Rod of covenant (shooting)	12"	Assault 1	5	-3	1	-
Staff of light (shooting)	12"	Assault 3	5	-2	1	-
Staff of the Destroyer (shooting)	18"	Assault 3	6	-3	2	-
Synaptic disintegrator	24"	Rapid Fire 1	4	0	1	This weapon may target a CHARACTER even if it is not the closest enemy unit. Each time you roll a wound roll of 6+ for this weapon, the target suffers a mortal wound in addition to any other damage.
Tachyon arrow	120"	Assault 1	10	-5	D6	This weapon can only be used once per battle.
Tesla cannon	24"	Assault 3	6	0	1	Each hit roll of 6+ with this weapon causes 3 hits instead of 1.
Tesla carbine	24"	Assault 2	5	0	1	Each hit roll of 6+ with this weapon causes 3 hits instead of 1.
Tesla destructor	24"	Assault 4	7	0	1	Each hit roll of 6+ with this weapon causes 3 hits instead of 1.
Tesla sphere	24"	Assault 5	7	0	1	Each hit roll of 6+ with this weapon causes 3 hits instead of 1.
Transdimensional beamer	12"	Heavy D3	4	-3	1	Each time you roll a wound roll of 6+ for this weapon, the target suffers a mortal wound in addition to any other damage.
Twin heavy gauss cannon	36"	Heavy 2	9	-4	D6	-
Twin tesla destructor	24"	Assault 8	7	0	1	Each hit roll of 6+ with this weapon causes 3 hits instead of 1.

MELEE WEAPONS

WEAPON	RANGE	TYPE	S	AP	D	ABILITIES
Automaton claws	Melee	Melee	User	-2	D3	-
Crackling tendrils	Melee	Melee	User	-4	D6	-
Eldritch Lance (melee)	Melee	Melee	User	-2	1	-
Empathic Obliterator	Melee	Melee	+2	-1	D3	If a **CHARACTER** is slain by an attack from this weapon, each unit within 6" (friend or foe) that is from the same Faction as the slain character suffers D3 mortal wounds.
Feeder mandibles	Melee	Melee	User	0	1	If the target's Toughness is higher than this attack's Strength, this weapon always wounds the target on a wound roll of 5+.
Flayer claws	Melee	Melee	User	0	1	You can re-roll failed wound rolls for this weapon.
Hyperphase sword	Melee	Melee	User	-3	1	-
Massive forelimbs	Melee	Melee	User	-1	D3	-
Rod of covenant (melee)	Melee	Melee	User	-3	1	-
Scythe of the Nightbringer	Melee	Melee	*	-4	D6	This weapon wounds on a 2+, unless it is targeting a **VEHICLE**, in which case it has a Strength characteristic of 7.
Staff of light (melee)	Melee	Melee	User	-2	1	-
Staff of the Destroyer (melee)	Melee	Melee	User	-3	2	-
Staff of Tomorrow	Melee	Melee	User	-3	D3	You can re-roll failed hit rolls for this weapon.
Star-god fists	Melee	Melee	User	-4	3	-
Vicious claws	Melee	Melee	User	-1	1	-
Voidblade	Melee	Melee	User	-3	1	-
Warscythe	Melee	Melee	+2	-4	2	-
Whip coils	Melee	Melee	User	0	1	If the bearer is slain in the Fight phase before it has made its attacks, leave the model where it is. When its unit is chosen to fight in that phase, it can do so as normal. Once it has done so, remove the model from the battlefield.

OTHER WARGEAR

WARGEAR	ABILITIES
Phylactery	A model with a phylactery regains D3 lost wounds at the beginning of your turn, rather than 1, from their Living Metal ability.
Resurrection orb	If a model has a resurrection orb, once per battle, immediately after you have made your Reanimation Protocols rolls, you can make Reanimation Protocol rolls for models from a friendly <DYNASTY> INFANTRY unit within 3" of the model.